GAURAV KEERTHI

THINK SPEAK WIN

DISCOVER the art of DEBATE

With a foreword by
Dr Vivian Balakrishnan

The author's proceeds from the sale of this book will go to the Debate Association (Singapore), a non-profit organisation, to help them reach out to even more students.

Published by Marshall Cavendish Editions
An imprint of Marshall Cavendish International
1 New Industrial Road, Singapore 536196

Other Marshall Cavendish Offices:
Marshall Cavendish International. PO Box 65829, London EC1P 1NY, UK • Marshall Cavendish Corporation. 99 White Plains Road, Tarrytown NY 10591-9001, USA • Marshall Cavendish International (Thailand) Co Ltd. 253 Asoke, 12th Flr, Sukhumvit 21 Road, Klongtoey Nua, Wattana, Bangkok 10110, Thailand • Marshall Cavendish (Malaysia) Sdn Bhd, Times Subang, Lot 46, Subang Hi-Tech Industrial Park, Batu Tiga, 40000 Shah Alam, Selangor Darul Ehsan, Malaysia.

National Library Board, Singapore Cataloguing-in-Publication Data
Keerthi, Gaurav, 1979–
Think Speak Win: Discover the Art of Debate / Gaurav Keerthi; with a foreword by Vivian Balakrishnan. – Singapore : Marshall Cavendish Editions, c2011.
p. cm.
ISBN : 978-981-4328-84-5 (Trade edition)
1. Debates and debating. I. Title.
PN4181
808.53 -- dc22 OCN700977978

Cover design by Steven Tan
Printed in Singapore by Fabulous Printers

For Peggy,
who graciously allows me to pretend to be
the better debater. ***xxy***

CONTENTS

FOREWORD

One of the more fortuitous turns in my life was the lack of an English teacher in Secondary One. Consequently, my classmates and I had a series of relief teachers who decided to organise debating sessions for us instead of routine formal lessons. Perhaps it involved less preparatory work on their part. Nevertheless, these weekly class debates gave all of us, even those of us who were naturally shy and reserved, access to a whole new way of thinking and using language to communicate and convince. In retrospect, the art of debate is probably just as essential as the ability to read.

Debating has made an enormous difference to my life journey. I have learnt to appreciate differences of opinion, the precision of logic, the elegance of expression and the power of persuasion. All these elements have been invaluable in my journey as a doctor, administrator and minister.

I have, of course, also discovered that real life is not just a debate. Very often, difficult decisions and painful choices have to be made. Occasionally, arriving at a consensus is better than a bitter clash of ideas, especially when there are strong emotions at play. It is not just about winning a theoretical argument, but exercising judgment to discern the right choice, to mobilise people and to be held accountable for consequences. Nevertheless, the discipline and methodology of debating are still essential attributes for a successful life.

I am pleased that Gaurav Keerthi has distilled the essentials of debating so well in this concise but comprehensive book. I read every page myself, and found good, practical advice. I would certainly recommend this book to anyone keen to commence or pursue a journey in debating.

Happy debating!

DR VIVIAN BALAKRISHNAN
Minister for Community Development, Youth and Sports

PREFACE

Discovering debate changed my life.

I have been debating, coaching, lecturing, and judging for over 16 years now. When I started, debating didn't come naturally – I took a few years to find my footing, slowly gain confidence, understand how to analyse issues, and present them to an audience in an interesting and persuasive way. There were no books or videos to guide me back then, so I just kept practising. When I finally got the hang of it towards the end of my schooling life, things started to click. My new-found confidence and analytical skills helped me get into my dream university, helped me win one of the most prestigious scholarships, and gave me the skills I need to excel in the working world. Debate holds a very special place in my heart and my life, because it transformed me. I have spent many years trying to provide that same opportunity to young students all around me. It has been difficult to find time to write this book, but if debate can have the same life-transforming effect on other young students, I believe it is worth the effort.

Debating offers important skills for success: Critical analysis (think), Communication (speak), and Confidence (win).

These "Three Cs" are considered to be the key capabilities and skills that companies look for in their new hires, and that top universities look for in their potential students. The reasons for this are plentiful and obvious: Someone who can think deeply and independently about a problem and come up with solutions, then communicate that solution persuasively to others, while being perceived as confident and sure-footed, is definitely a good candidate for a top job or a spot in a prestigious university. Debaters are also well-read, because they have to understand the background of many issues in current affairs in order to debate them effectively. It is little wonder then that many of the most successful people in the world – whether from the business, academic or political spheres – have had some debate training in their school days. In Singapore, debaters are well-represented on the list of past President's Scholars.

Debaters tend to have more balanced opinions because they are trained to see both sides of every issue.

Every debater knows that they may be asked to argue for or against the death penalty or abortion in their next debate – they don't get to pick their sides – and they must thus be able to understand the reasons and evidence for and against those controversial topics. This forced dual-perspective on contentious issues requires debaters to step outside their own viewpoints and consider the possible counter-arguments. They also learn that any view they hold should be substantiated with logic and evidence if possible – and this usually prevents debaters from holding illogical and biased opinions that are derived from stereotypes or other irrational considerations. This type of thinking stays with them for life. Debaters tend to always analyse both sides of an issue before making their decisions, and thus are able to come to more balanced and rational perspectives.

Debaters prefer healthy discussion to aggressive arguments.
Debate is part of the human impulse to communicate thoughts, opinions, views, and beliefs. Debate can connect two people who are divided on a topic. Debaters prefer healthy arguments rather than bitter emotional battles. When people are unable to express their opinions in words well enough, they often resort to emotion or aggression. Go online now and read any forum in which people disagree about something – Are Macs better than PCs? Should schools teach safe-sex? Should homosexual marriage be legalised? – and see how long it takes before the forum degenerates into illogical assertions, name-calling, and mud-slinging. There are some countries famous for their having parliaments erupt into vicious yelling and even fist-fighting when two opposing politicians are unable to discuss their disagreements maturely. I think it is in society's best interests that we teach people how to debate complex issues in a civilised manner, so there is no need to resort to the uncivilised.

> "*Difference of opinion leads to inquiry, and inquiry to truth.*"
>
> — THOMAS JEFFERSON

Anybody can learn to debate if they want to. It is not a sport reserved for the academic elite. Don't be scared of debaters!
Debate is not a recent phenomenon. It did not begin with politicians or Ivy League students. It is impossible to give a definite history of debate. My suspicion is that debate even preceded formal language – that when cavemen gathered to evaluate how to hunt using the spear, they must have compared the different tactics and somehow "debated" the pros and cons. Somewhere along the way, debate was hijacked by the classrooms of the best schools, and burdened

with elaborate rules, special terms, and a manner of speech that only other fellow debaters could understand. Debate became so complex that it left behind the people who mattered – us. This is wrong. Debate should appeal to and be understandable by the average man on the street.

Debate should not be taught to students just to win competitions; it should be taught because it is important for the students' life-long development, for the same reasons we teach students maths and science. I have seen students from weaker schools do well in competitive debate given the right training, and I have seen how their self-confidence improved dramatically as a direct result. Debate can and should be taught across all schools, as part of the core curriculum. Singapore's Ministry of Education has recently made debate a "core skill" for all students in primary and secondary school.

There are very few books that teach you how to think faster and speak better. This book aims to fix that.

There are many books on "Persuasive Speaking," but those books fail to get to the root of persuasion because they only teach you how to *speak* persuasively, but they don't teach you how to also *think* persuasively. Those books assume that you have already written a compelling, analytical, intelligent, well-researched speech, but you have difficulty delivering that content to an audience. That is rarely the case. Most people have difficulty communicating because they have difficulty thinking of what to say as well as how to say it. Most people face difficulties with everyday speaking – whether they are being questioned at a business meeting, or being grilled by a scholarship interview panel. Public-speaking or persuasive-speaking books are not very useful in these situations, because "visualising your audience naked" is not going to help you analyse the tough question and come up with an intelligent response or counter-proposal!

There are indeed some books on debating, but these books often focus on extremely technical advice, specific to certain competitive debate formats (mainly American). They contain cryptic debaterese jargon such as "deficit disads," "attitudinal inherency," "fiats," "kritiks," or "tiered sub-contentions" – terms that mean nothing to most intelligent people. There are no books that I know of that teach the key concepts and skills of debating from scratch, free of technical jargon.

This book aims to close both those gaps. It introduces readers to the basic skills of debating in an easy, non-technical way. These skills are as useful in a debate competition as they are in everyday life and conversation. The last chapter of this book will show you how to achieve success by using "debate-thinking" in your daily life.

Debate as an activity can advance issues, unveil false arguments and misperceptions, and clarify complex topics.

I think debate is the first step towards improving our world. Before we embark on any course of action, before we make a decision on any morally challenging policy, before we change laws, we must evaluate the pros and cons of the choice that we (as a society) are about to make. We *must* debate. We must pit the opposing arguments against each other and see which prevails in the contest of ideas and logic and evidence. In the process, we uncover those ideas that are false, and cast light on areas previously in the dark. Debate helps people separate fact from fiction, because the opposing team will quickly point out any lies that are told. And where we cannot ourselves participate in the debate, we must be able to analyse and dissect the arguments and evidence that the politicians make in the senate or parliament as our representatives, to satisfy ourselves that they are making the right decisions for the country. Democracies are founded upon the "marketplace of ideas" and depend upon the voting masses to listen closely to the political debate of their countries and vote according to which side they prefer. When people do not understand those debates, they may become disaffected, apathetic, and resign themselves to the hands of politicians (or worse yet, vote on irrational grounds). Being able to understand, participate, and contribute to the political process in a meaningful way is a fundamental right of any person in a democracy. Too few people have been taught those critical debate skills.

This book is meant to give everyone a chance to open up, speak up, and make a difference. Good luck.

THINK
SPEAK
WIN

"I used to think one of the most powerful individuals in America was the person who could select the annual high-school debate topic. Think of the power – to set the agenda, and determine what millions of high school students will study, read about, think about, talk about with friends, discuss with their teachers, and debate with their parents and siblings over dinner."

— DONALD RUMSFELD,
in his testimony to the
"9/11" Commission

1

WHAT IS DEBATE

IN 2003 AND 2004, high school students across America were required to debate whether they were losing the "War on Terror," and whether politicians should oversee the intelligence community. As Rumsfeld's comment shows, debate is a powerful tool to unravel complex and controversial issues. In a nutshell, a debate requires a topic, some debaters, and few pre-arranged rules governing the format and structure of the debate.

Debate topics

A topic focuses the debate to a single issue.

A debate without a fixed topic would essentially have no end. Each issue would lead to another one, and the conversation would never be able to find any sort of resolution – which would be very frustrating for an audience (and the debaters). A debate might start on the death penalty, then discuss criminals in general, then discuss religious views on killing, then discuss different religious ideologies in general, and wander even further astray from there.

Having a clear, specific debate topic allows people to focus their attention and analysis on the single issue at hand, and thereby educate the audience on the pros and cons of that issue or policy.

A good debate topic divides societal opinion.

The world we live in is full of grey areas – issues that have no black-and-white "correct" answers. The death penalty. Abortion. Affirmative action. These and many other issues continue to divide public opinion. There are good arguments both for and against these policies. Governments sometimes change their policies when the balance of societal opinion shifts (slowly, over time) from one side to the other. Regular debate on such topics is the only way to keep the audience educated about the pros and cons of each issue, so that they can cast an informed and well-balanced vote for the policies that they think are best. Without debate, people may not get exposed to the counter-arguments and contrary views, and may thus cast uninformed votes.

Controversial topics are all around us.

Newspaper headlines are often perfect natural topics for a debate: "Government announces lower taxes for locals." Is this the right thing to do, to help the local populace? Or would it discourage foreigners from coming here and thereby stall economic development?

Philosophy asks us probing moral questions: Should we have the power to decide life and death by giving the courts the option of a death penalty? Or is the death penalty too draconian a measure for a civilised society? Should the issue be decided by principles, or should it be judged by the effectiveness of the death penalty in reducing crime rates?

Even our mundane daily lives offer plenty of debatable issues: Should you go overseas for university, or stay near home? What are the merits and demerits of each option? Even though it seems like a "small" issue, it is still something that would benefit from a robust debate, so that you can make an informed decision.

Debaters

We are all debaters.

If you believe you have never debated before, you are wrong. We are all debaters – some of us have debated competitively, while others have debated informally with friends or peers. Working adults often have to persuade their bosses or colleagues on the merits of their ideas, and sometimes have to defend their ideas against criticism. That's debating. Children, when told that they cannot do something, often ask the very pointed question, "Why not?" That's an invitation to debate. We have all debated before, and we all engage in little debates every day.

Debaters argue for their side of the case.

Much like lawyers who argue for their client's case, debaters argue for their side of the case. Having a specific "side" to be on allows you to explore all the arguments and evidence in favour of that particular side, and force you to defend that perspective. When paired with an opposing debater, the clash of arguments and ideas will necessarily result in a more robust analysis of the issue at hand.

Sometimes, students are required to debate both sides on their own – that is, they are required to explore the case for *and* against the topic, within the same speech or essay. It is often impossible to analyse an issue without any sort of side or opinion. If you simply list the arguments for and against a topic without any personal perspective as to which arguments are more credible and which are more well-substantiated, your analysis may be very superficial and shallow. So, even if you are required to argue both for and against a topic, you should always have a clear perspective as to which side you are more aligned with, so that you can analyse the opposing arguments more critically and support your own arguments with more conviction.

Format and structure

Debates need a formal pre-arranged structure.

Without an agreed and pre-arranged structure, an intellectual debate quickly gives way to a rowdy argument. This happens regularly in some political situations, where a heated discussion turns into an all-out shouting match, and ultimately provides no useful illumination on the issue that caused the disagreement in the first place. Voters don't benefit, and both politicians often come out of the argument with tarnished reputations.

Rules are put in place to give each speaker an equal and fair opportunity to present his side of the story or issue. Courtrooms have complicated procedures for how lawyers may present their case, and more advanced democracies have rules on how their cabinet or parliament may debate issues.

Debates require at least two opposing sides.

This is the most basic ingredient of any debate format: There should be at least two opposing sides. Some formats have more than two teams on each side (that is, two teams argue for the topic, and two teams against it); some formats allow for more than two sides (e.g., in political candidate show-downs, where each candidate presents his or her own side to a complex policy issue). However, the minimum for a debate to occur is two sides. The two sides must disagree on some part of the issue – otherwise it is not a debate. The debate should focus on the disagreement, so that the audience understands where the differences are and can make an assessment of which side is more convincing.

Debates are conducted in front of a judge and an audience.
Without a judge, there would be no external and unbiased view on how the debaters performed and who "won" the issues. Each debater would enter the debate convinced that his arguments are correct, and leave the debate with the same opinion. A judge is important because he provides an external assessment of the quality of arguments raised. In later chapters, we will explore the role of the judge further.

Although it is not mandatory, it is customary for debates to be held in front of an audience. The audience listens to all the opposing arguments, and they form their own opinions based on what they have heard. They may align themselves entirely with one side or the other, or they may form their own opinions from a hybrid of all the arguments raised during the debate. This process is known as the "Hegelian dialectic" (after Georg Wilhelm Friedrich Hegel, the German philosopher), where one side expresses their *thesis* in the form of an argument, the opposing side presents the *antithesis* in the form of counter-arguments, and then the audience forms their own opinion by resolving the conflict between the two sides with their own view – the *synthesis*. This thesis-antithesis-synthesis process is one of the educational outcomes of debating in front of an audience.

Sometimes the audience is the judge.
In political debates especially, the millions of voters who watch the debates effectively decide the winner. There is no assigned "judge" for the debate, but the audience is given the power to vote for the winner, either through a national election or through post-debate polls. This is sometimes replicated at student debates, where electronic voting systems are becoming increasingly popular.

Debates are an extremely powerful and effective way to educate an audience, and to prompt people to think more deeply about the complexities of controversial issues.

2

DEFINING THE OBJECTIVE

"So long as I'm the president, my measure of success is victory – and success."

— GEORGE W. BUSH, on Iraq

HOW EXACTLY DOES one measure success, if the definition of success is – also – success? This quote shows us how important meaningful definitions are, and how a bad definition can lead to a horrible speech. Before you talk about any topic, you must first understand what the objective is, and define it clearly. Making a long passionate speech without a good grasp of what the topic means is a recipe for disaster, not victory.

Set the context

Why is this topic being debated now?

All debate topics stem from real-world issues. Explaining the context will add relevance to the topic, and bring it alive for the audience and the judges. In order to set the context correctly, you must of course know how and why this topic is important in the world today. You must thus have a good grasp of current affairs and be very well-read and widely read. Make it a point to read the daily news and current-affairs journals. Be curious about all subjects, and browse websites such as Wikipedia for introductions to topics you are unfamiliar with.

Background research is critical.

If it is an *event-specific* topic (for example the success of post-war reconstruction in Iraq), it is critical that you do detailed research to understand the background issues and the status quo. Otherwise, you will not have the necessary material to defend your case.

Current affairs can impact age-old philosophical debates.

Debate topics can be seen as part of an even wider discussion of a broader concept or philosophical discussion about humanity. You should read up on philosophy to understand some perennial human concerns. Do the means ever justify the ends? Should the state dictate moral standards for its citizens? What is the value of life? What does the justice system aim to achieve? Philosophers have grappled with many such issues for centuries, and these issues keep cropping up in debates and conversation. Some arguments for such "evergreen" topics can be prepared well in advance. However, even these arguments evolve over time (with changing societal views) and some new arguments arise because of recent news or changes in societal norms.

> *"When the facts change, I change my mind. What do you do, sir?"*
>
> — JOHN MAYNARD KEYNES,
> British economist, responding to a criticism that he had changed his position on monetary policy

New events and discoveries cause arguments to evolve.

Even for more generic philosophical debate topics (such as censorship, prostitution, gambling), it is still vital to link the topic to recent events and set the context. Sometimes new facts arise that completely change the assumptions for your case, so it is very, *very* important to be up-to-date in your research for all issues.

Motion: The internet should be censored.

If this debate had taken place before 2001, the context would have been quite different. Parents were afraid of the unrestricted nature of the internet and how their children might access pornography or violence; racial-tolerance activists were worried about the emergence of "hate sites" on the web. Those would thus have been the central issues of the debate. Today, however, in a post-9/11 world where terrorism threatens peace and stability, any debate on the topic would be incomplete unless the teams addressed the danger of fundamentalist or "terrorist training" websites that allow extremists to recruit more people to their cause. Terrorism itself may not be new, but the use of the internet for terrorism (such as uploading videos of gruesome torture of their captives) is certainly an issue that would not have been debated before. Likewise, social networking websites have also grown exponentially in recent years, and many are concerned that they need to be regulated because they may expose unwitting youngsters to sexual predators.

Simple, clear, specific definitions

Nobody likes complex definitions. Keep it simple.

Don't make it a complicated or unwieldy definition; don't be a smart-alec and twist the meaning of the words. People dislike this in normal conversations, and judges certainly don't appreciate it in a debate. You should present the *plain and intended meaning of the motion*, to debate the intended "spirit" of the topic according to the *man-on-the-street's interpretation*. If a particular word in the topic has more than one meaning, stick to the most commonly used meaning or the one that would make the most sense in the context of the debate topic. Later on, we will discuss exactly what qualifies as an unfair definition, but suffice it to say that any attempt to warp the debate by re-defining the key terms in an "unconventional" or "unexpected" way will be penalised. Avoid "clever" definitions that require rhetorical cartwheels to explain. Keep it simple.

Motion: Children should not be allowed on the web unsupervised.

Negative example: Oh, wouldn't it be so funny if you played a trick on the opposition team by defining the word "web" as spiderwebs, instead of the World Wide Web? That would catch them unprepared, and then you could run a clever case about how spiderwebs are for spiders, not children! Haha! No, that would not be funny, and you would not win any debates that way.

Dictionaries don't always know best.

You should never rely on a dictionary *alone* to define a debate motion, because dictionaries lack common sense and context. Dictionaries provide literal, exact definitions, without any understanding of how the surrounding words in the motion may impact their meaning. To avoid reliance on dictionary definitions, you should try to build a strong vocabulary (and don't be afraid to ask for the meaning of words that you are unsure of). It is less embarrassing to ask for the meaning than to mistakenly assume it means something else and thence build an irrelevant case.

Some phrases in a motion refer to specific terminology or to phrases that have meanings that cannot be found in a dictionary. Often, a simple internet search for the topic will reveal any terms with specific contextual meanings. Reading widely also helps. If it's still vague, ask the organiser of the debate – it may be a cultural-specific term (local vernacular or slang) that you are not familiar with.

For example, "crimes against humanity" do not refer to "unlawful offences" against the "quality of being humane" even though that may be the literal dictionary definition. Rather, the phrase refers to a specific definition of the phrase by the United Nations (under the International Criminal Court), denoting large-scale persecution or acts of atrocity against a body of people, including war crimes and genocide. Likewise, "green terrorism" obviously does not refer to terrorist action against things painted green, but to environmental extremism. "Friends of the Earth," "coalition of the willing," along with many other phrases, all have meanings that would be incomplete or totally wrong if only a dictionary were used.

"It depends on what the definition of 'is' is."

— BILL CLINTON,
arguing at his impeachment
trial that he "is" not involved
with Monica Lewinsky

Know the aim of the debate

Most importantly, what do you need to prove or disprove?

Debate topics are phrased to be deliberately contentious – you are always required to explain or prove something to win. To this end, there will always be particular "trigger" words in the motion that indicate what is required of each side. We will see in this section how these trigger words can help you determine whether you should emphasise on whether something is true or false (Debates of Fact), whether something should be done (Debates of Opinion), how it should be done (Debates of Policy), or whether something is likely to happen in the future (Debates of Trend and Analysis).

> *"Furious activity is no substitute for understanding."*
>
> — H.H. WILLIAMS

Debates of Fact: Is X true or false?

These debates require you to prove whether your side believes the topic is factually accurate or not. Trigger words in the motion that indicate this class of debates include "is," "are," "was," and other words that are in the present or past tense.

Sample motions

- Exams are a waste of time.
- Chivalry is dead.
- Globalisation has done more harm than good.
- The UN has failed.
- George W. Bush was wrong to invade Iraq.
- Multi-national corporations control the world.

For these debates, the burden of proof is on the proposition to (1) clearly define what are the evaluative criteria for the end state, and then (2) establish why the world is – or is not – in that situation. Consider the motion, "Exams are a waste of time." The proposition must first define what constitutes a "waste of time" (and to whom) and then establish why exams fall into that category. This is subjective – there is no correct *factual* answer to this question. The key to these debates is to select facts and interpret the points to justify your analysis. Oppositions must do the same, but in reverse. There is no right or wrong answer, even in debates of fact. Debate topics are always open to interpretation and it is your *opinion* on the truth of the topic that you are defending. That is, does your team *think* that exams are a waste of time or not?

The critical point to remember is that you are *not* being asked for whether exams should be more highly valued; these motions do not care about how the outcome should/could/would have been, but what it actually *is* today.

> *"During my service with the United States Congress, I took the initiative in creating the Internet."*
>
> – AL GORE, taking some liberties with fact

Debates of Opinion: Why should we do X?

For these debates, the proposition must provide reasons and evidence why they support or disagree with the topic. In a conversation, if somebody asks whether the government should or must do something (for example, allow euthanasia), they are asking for your opinion on *why* they should – or should not. The mechanics of the implementation (how the government will legalise and regulate euthanasia) are of secondary importance in this conversation or debate, but should still be thought through. Other trigger words that can indicate debates of this sort are "could," "might," "must," "need to," "ought to," "should," "would."

Sample motions

- Sportsmen are paid too much/are overpaid.
- This house would support affirmative action for university students.
- Voluntary euthanasia should be allowed/legalised.
- We regret the power of the free press.
- This house supports trial by jury.
- This house laments that we have no more heroes.
- This house regrets that free trade is impossible.
- We suffer from a lack of national identity.
- The world dreads the rise of feminism.

Debates of opinion may be indicated by *subjective* terms or *superlatives* (most, furthest), or the adverb "too" (too much, too far), such as in the motions "Sportsmen are paid too much" or "Sportsmen are overpaid." This motion demands a proposition to explain *why* they think sportsmen are paid too much.

Motions that use *emotive* words such as "dreads," "laments," "regrets," "supports," etc., also indicate that the team must prove reasons why that particular emotion is justified. For example, "The world *regrets* the re-election of George W. Bush" is a debate that requires the team to analyse *why* one would have cause to regret his second presidential term.

Debates of Policy: How should we do X?

These debates require the team to recommend a course of action to deal with the issue. The trigger words for these motions are "legalistic" trigger words such as "ban," "prohibit," and "abolish."

Sample motions

- This house would ban advertising for all alcoholic drinks.
- We would prohibit the use of underweight fashion models.
- We should ban violent cartoons.
- Schools should abolish exams.
- Smoking in public places should be banned.

The proposition must normally first establish the *why* by giving compelling reasons for the topic, and then explain how the proposed measure is feasible and best solves the problem. For example, "Smoking in public places should be *banned*" asks the proposition to first provide compelling reasons why smoking should be banned, and then explain how their proposed course of action would work. We will discuss how to establish a strong "policy" – which is a model of how your solution can be implemented – in the next chapter.

Debates of Trend and Analysis: How will the future be?

These topics straddle debates of fact and debates of opinion, in that you must first examine the facts, and then give your postulation of whether this indicates a trend towards the future scenario described in the motion. You must do more than just make wild speculations. The trigger words for these motions are usually related to time or chronology: words like "will" or "could," or verbs in the future tense.

Sample motions

- Communism will die.
- This house believes in peace in our time.
- The age of the printed page is over (implies *from today on*).
- The environmental movement is destined to fail (implies *in the future*).

These debates do not require you to explain or defend whether that outcome is a beneficial scenario to anybody – that is, you are usually *not* required to provide your opinion on whether the outcome is preferred or not. For example, "This house believes that Communism *will* die" requires you to determine whether Communism (as a political system) has been on the decline, and whether or not the last remaining countries are likely to give it up as well (and you may want to prove that once it has "died," it is not going to see a resurgence ever again because it is not compatible with the future world and will thus stay "dead").

Evaluation criteria

What do you need to prove in order to win?

In the American presidential race of 2009 between John McCain and Barack Obama, many voters were undecided and wanted to vote for the "best" candidate. The problem was in defining "best" in this context. What criteria should voters use? If you believed that good grades and high IQ make the candidate "best" then perhaps Obama – who graduated *magna cum laude* from Harvard Law School – would have been the better choice. However, if you felt that political experience mattered more, then McCain's long history as a U.S. senator would make him the "best" candidate for you. There are obviously hundreds of other factors that would have to be considered, like how the candidates stood on various issues and how they performed in the run-up to the election. Many websites tried to compile such comparison charts so that voters could decide "for themselves" which candidate was best for them. In this very simplistic comparison with a limited set of criteria, the voter would probably have picked Obama.

	Barack Obama	John McCain
Education	• B.A., Columbia University • J.D., Harvard Law School, *magna cum laude*	• B.S., United States Naval Academy • National War College
Political experience	• U.S. senator since 2005 • Illinois state senator since 1997	• U.S. senator since 1986
Charisma	• Great orator	• Good speaker

Debates are judged according to a proposed set of criteria.

In a debate, each team tries to convince the judge and audience that it has the "best" case. The judge and audience then have to evaluate which team presents the better solution to the problem defined in the motion, by comparing the two solutions side by side on a set of criteria. Just like in the table above between Obama and McCain, you should identify a set of criteria that you want the judge to use to evaluate the solutions provided by both sides, and pick the best one. Teams should always propose the criteria explicitly, rather than leaving it implicit or letting the judge come up with his own.

Your team's burden of proof is to prove that your case is better – based on the set of criteria.

In a debate, the same process applies – the problem you intend to solve is contained within the aim of the motion or topic. If you want the judge to think that your solution is better, you must compare your case against the other team's case on each criteria and show why yours is better. The process of establishing what your team aims to prove is often known as setting the burden of proof or the onus for your side. The burden of proof must contain the checklist of criteria for evaluation – you must let the adjudicator and audience know how to fairly compare and contrast the two team's cases.

Develop a fair and thorough set of criteria

To be *fair*, the criteria must not be biased or judgmental. They should be based on neutral, objective standards that require minimal value-judgments. For example, a fair set of criteria to evaluate the quality of a restaurant could be based on what the Michelin Guide uses in their recognition of top restaurants – the quality of ingredients, the skill in preparing them and in combining flavours, the level of creativity, the consistency of culinary standards and the value for money. An unfair criterion would be "which restaurant my parents like better" because that may be biased and subjective... unless your parents run the Michelin Guide, of course. You can research online for the criteria used by professional agencies that give out awards in the area that you are debating. What factors do they consider?

> *"I desire what is good. Therefore, everyone who does not agree with me is a traitor."*
>
> — KING GEORGE III,
> defining (somewhat biased)
> criteria for identifying traitors

To be *thorough*, the criteria should consider the impact to all sectors or individuals who may be affected by the topic, not just the ones on your side of the topic. For example, a thorough set of criteria to evaluate the impact of banning smoking should include the impact it has on the government, the tobacco industry, the non-smokers, and also the smoking populace. Some teams try and exclude the smoking populace from this motion because it's "easier" to prove that a smoking ban is beneficial if we ignore the interests of smokers. Clearly, this is not a thorough evaluation because smokers are still citizens with rights too, and their views must be considered.

Show that your case is in the best interests of all involved.

In developing the criteria for motions of principle or policy (to prove that there is a moral and practical need), you may list and explain the various costs and benefits that arise from the policy and then do a simple direct comparison to see which policy meets more items on this checklist. In all debates, you must prove that the chosen course of action or decision to be supported is in the best interests of some groups of people (more on this in the next chapter).

Motion: We should allow voluntary euthanasia.

Your team could prove on both the principle (the *why*) and practical (the *how*) level that allowing voluntary euthanasia is (1) best for the patient in the short-run, (2) best for the family of the patient, (3) best for the medical profession (based on the aims of the Hippocratic Oath), and (4) best for society in the long-run. Almost instantly you can see your case being outlined, and points emerging clearly. The power of a clear setup and definition is obvious — a team may have won half the battle if they are able to understand the topic and define the burden of proof clearly.

Break up subjective or ambiguous terms in the motion into clearer, more easily measurable components.

If a topic contains a clearly subjective term – a term that can be interpreted in many ways or by many different standards, with no "black and white" answer – you should define the term in more objective terms and then break it down into "subcomponents" to evaluate each step of the policy or principle.

> **Motion**: Examinations have failed us.
>
> The subjective word in the motion is "failed." Different people interpret the word differently, so you should analyse and explain clearly what constitutes a "failure" for this debate topic's context. You could say that something should be considered a failure if it fails to meet its own aims (in this case, to assess a student's ability in a subject), and that they have failed to meet the aims of the education system (to nurture and encourage true learning and curiosity among students), and so on.

Draw a "line in the sand" for topics about acceptable limits.

Some motions ask the teams to make a qualitative assessment about the scale of something (that is, to what extent is the situation true), and where the subjective limits should be. This is often known in debate circles as *drawing a line in the sand*. Teams must state clearly what is within acceptable limits and what crosses that line and is too much (or, depending on the phrasing of the motion, what is too violent, too fast, etc.).

> **Motion**: Sportsmen are paid too much.
>
> The key concern is how much pay is too much pay? How do we normally determine how much pay a professional is worth? Is their pay "too much" because we feel like they don't deserve it (based on their job responsibilities or impact on society), because they don't need it

(their extravagant lifestyles are an unnecessary distraction from their sporting careers) or because the free market is over-paying them due to other factors? How else can we determine when someone is paid "too much"?

For complex motions, build up your criteria progressively.
Some motions are very long: "We should do Course of Action A because of Principle B," or "We should achieve Objective A through Course of Action B." The team must define both A and B in these cases, and then explain the criteria and burden of proof.

Motion: We should achieve gender equality by affirmative action in university rather than the workplace.
The proposition is required to prove a few things progressively:
1. That we have not yet achieved gender equality in society and it is desirable to expedite the process using government policy tools.
2. That affirmative action in university is effective (as opposed to other measures, such as societal campaigns).
3. That affirmative action in universities is better than in the workplace for the goal of achieving gender equality.

There are other ways to break it up, and it is possible to lump (2) and (3) together to a single stage but it is usually more convincing if you can break it down into smaller parts.

Determine the scope

Should you widen or narrow the scope of the debate?
A team will never be expected to prove that the motion will hold true under every conceivable circumstance in every place on earth without exception for all time. A team needs to define and determine the scope of situations under which the topic is true, or

exclude some particular unique scenarios from consideration. This is a tricky business. You must balance the desire to limit the scope of the debate with the need to have a fair and thorough debate. Judges and opposition teams understand this as well. It is important for the proposition to state upfront what the *prerequisite conditions* for their case are. You can thus narrow the scope of the debate to rule out certain cases from the scope of the debate, and give good reasons why you wish to limit the scope.

Specific motions need specific scopes.

In motions that are set on very specific areas, the team is expected to narrow the scope to just those specific areas. Specific motions should be debated specifically; even if general principles are used to support the logic, the scope of your general principles should be made relevant to the specific topic of the debate.

> **Motion**: The United States should pull all combat troops out of the Middle East within one year.
> The motion should be limited to just that specific issue; there is no reason to bring in broader questions about whether a foreign military should ever be stationed in another country as a principle, or whether military peacekeeping should ever be done by a foreign country in general. Even if you raise the general argument that military peacekeeping is always bad, you should relate your argument specifically to the topic of American troops in the Middle East.

Conversely, generalised motions need broad scopes.

The opposite applies for motions that are general, and expressed as statements of principle; you should not suddenly limit the scope to one particular example or specific case. An extreme and unfair instance of wrongly applying a narrow scope to a broad topic would be *time-setting* or *place-setting* (covered later in this chapter).

Motion: Our government should do more to help the poor.

You should not limit the entire debate to whether or not regressive taxation policies are the best way to help the poor—this is a debate about the general principle of whether governments should be more "welfarist" in general, not about the feasibility of specific measures.

Sometimes, it is necessary and justified to narrow the scope.

Some debates are so wide that they can be interpreted in a thousand different ways. It would thus be impossible to have a meaningful debate unless both teams agreed to narrow down the topic to a few scenarios and then debate on those common grounds. However, you can and should only narrow the scope if it meets the following conditions:

Only present clarifications that are required for your reasonable case to hold true.

That is, if you do not exclude those other areas from the debate, you cannot reasonably prove your case. Some teams like to have a preset list of conditions to impose on the debate – just in case. These "drift-net" or "blanket" clarifications often have no bearing whatsoever on the case you will be presenting, and thus should *not* be issued. Some teams love to state that their solution will not be a panacea to the problem. This is already understood and obvious – if there *was* a panacea to the problem, it would have been adopted across the world already!

You must substantiate why the scope should be narrowed.

The most common clarification that I have heard (used wrongly) is that the debate should be restricted to "First-World liberal democracies" – even in motions about Third-World problems, where the bulk of the evidence will obviously come from outside this scope. If you narrow the scope and then give evidence from outside your own scope, it will look very poor to the adjudicator. You must be able to explain why it is logical for the scope to be narrowed.

Motion: Voluntary euthanasia should be legalised.

In this debate, the scope should be limited to countries with properly functioning legal systems, so that errant doctors who commit murder in the guise of voluntary euthanasia are dealt with effectively, thereby preventing other doctors from abusing the system in place. This is a fair premise, and is a well-substantiated clarification. If the debate were to be extended to countries where doctors run amok and the law cannot stop them, then it is impossible to enforce any sort of punitive measures on a doctor, and also impossible to enforce any policy regarding voluntary euthanasia.

On a more fundamental level, it would probably make the entire debate irrelevant, because if there is no functioning legal system, then nobody would care what is allowed; they would just go ahead and do as they please! However, this clarification now allows you to scope your case only to the more developed countries, because only they would be within the scope of the debate. All the other benefits of developed societies (such as societal respect for the dignity of life, strong valuation for freedom of choice, high likelihood of adequate hospital facilities, etc.) can all be utilised in your case more easily.

The topic must allow you to limit the scope without conceding.

Some motions are deliberately phrased in absolute terms ("never," "always," etc.). While you may be allowed to limit the scope, there is a risk of *conceding* (accidentally losing the case) if you narrow the scope too much. The other team will claim that you are unfairly excluding viable cases and trying to define the topic unfairly. As shown in the example below, there is a big difference between proving that the motion is true for all viable cases, and (unfairly) narrowing the scope to exclude cases that you have difficulty rebutting.

Motion: We should never negotiate with terrorists.

If you tried to narrow the scope by claiming that you should only examine cases in which terrorists are making gunpoint demands, i.e., when they have hostages as bargaining chips, then implicitly you are saying that it is fine to negotiate with terrorists under any other circumstance (if they come to discuss issues non-violently, but they have not renounced violence as a method of operations). This is clearly a concession and may cause you to lose the debate.

Absolute terms (e.g., "always," "never") only require you to prove that the topic is true in principle for the viable cases.

Sometimes the topic is phrased in very contentious and dramatic ways so that it provokes a strong reaction. There is a difference between the motion "Examinations have failed us" and "Nobody should ever sit for exams again" – the latter motion is more dramatic, and includes certain absolute terms like "nobody" and "ever again." Clearly the topic is designed to polarise the teams so that one side argues that there is still some value in retaining exams for some people, while the other side must argue that there is no value in keeping exams as an option. However, does the team need to really prove that *nobody* in the entire planet should ever, ever sit for an exam? No. The team can set a criteria to prove that the motion is true (or false) for all *viable cases* – or conversely, that there are no viable exceptions.

Motion: State-provided primary school education should be made compulsory for all.

An example of an invalid (and utterly stupid) opposition case would be where the opposition talks about a *single* contrary example of some hypothetical child who was born in a vegetative state or with severe degenerative diseases and thus cannot be subjected to compulsory education — and thus defies the motion. Obviously that poor child will not have to go through primary school education, and it would be unfair and ridiculous of the opposition to expect the proposition to be held to the impossible task of literally proving that the education must be made compulsory for every living thing.

A more reasonable opposition case would be to explain that there are some *viable* exceptions — some groups who should be exempted from compulsory education even though they fit all the other conditions to attend a normal school. One example would be children whose parents wish to home-school them instead of sending them to state-based schools.

Avoid unfair definitions

Would the common person see your definition as unbiased?

If you stick to the first principle of definitions (Keep It Simple, Stupid!), you should be able to steer clear of unfair definitions. Nonetheless, it's good to be aware of when a definition may be considered unfair so that you can avoid them intentionally (or point them out if another team tries to use one on you in a debate!). The following are some basic types of *unfair definitions*.

A tautology is something that is made true by how the person defines it; it negates the possibility of any debate.

In a debate, this may come in the form of the criteria or onus from a proposition that sets up the winning parameters of the debate to be what the proposition has to prove, and thereby prevents the opposition from running any case at all.

Motion: Singapore should ban smoking.

The proposition states the team that should win the debate is the team that finds the best way to eliminate smoking as a problem in society. Essentially, this team has just rephrased the motion — a ban on smoking is the same thing as eliminating smoking from society. So what the proposition is really saying here is that the only way to win this debate is to agree that society must ban smoking. This is clearly unfair to the opposition and an example of a tautological definition.

Loading a definition with emotional baggage makes it biased.

When a team's choice of definition is "weighted" or "loaded" to evoke a natural "feeling" or emotive response against the other team, it makes a debate extremely difficult. Using emotive language or subjective terminology in your definitions only clouds the real issue further, so stick to the facts.

Motion: Abortion should be banned.

If a proposition defined abortion as "the intentional premeditated murder of unborn babies," it would obviously bias the debate more so than by defining it as "the termination of a foetus prior to birth."

Deliberately misinterpreting the motion is bad strategy.

Some teams try to deliberately add some nuance to the definition that tries to "trick" their opponents or allow them to run some other arguments that may not be relevant to the motion unless their "tricky" definition is accepted. In this case, when a team deliberately shifts the definition in order to suit some other prepared case (which can happen in a impromptu debate, to allow a team to run arguments for a slightly different prepared motion), this is known as "squirrelling" the definitions. Under the rules of the World Schools Debating Championships (WSDC), this is "the distortion of the definition to enable a team to argue a pre-prepared argument that it wishes to debate regardless of the motion actually set." This is a bad strategy, and illegal in many formats of debate.

Other teams try to define the topic in a different sense from the commonly understood interpretation (especially when a word has a double meaning), with the intention of throwing the opposition team off.

Motion: Marx would be proud of the internet.

In a particularly amusing debate on this motion, the proposition decided (unfairly, of course) that they would not use the common definition of Marx — that is, Karl Marx — and instead use Richard Marx (who sang "Right Here Waiting," a hit love ballad of the 90s). The proposition case was thus that one-hit wonders like Richard Marx were unable to sell their albums because all the other songs on the album were lousy, but the internet (and programs like iTunes) allowed Marx to sell his one hit song; hence he is happy that the internet has given him more market access than he would have otherwise enjoyed. Clearly the opposition was unprepared for such a radically different definition from what everybody expected, and argued that the more common definition should be Karl Marx.

Limiting the scope unfairly can lead to incomplete cases.

Most debate formats prevent you from deliberate *place-setting* (e.g., "This debate is only limited to cases from the eastern coast of England") and *time-setting* ("Our team's case will be true only for examples from the late 16th century"). Nevertheless, some teams try to sneak in some elements of these in the clarifications without explaining why these limitations are fair. In the worst case, if you limit the scope too much, your case may not prove the entire motion, and would thus be considered an incomplete case.

Note, however, that *some* debate formats allow, or even overtly encourage, time-setting and place-setting, to promote more "creative" interpretations of the principles in the debate.

Definitions must be consistent across all team members.

As a team, always ensure that all speakers are consistent in the way they use and understand the key terms of the debate. It is incredibly awkward if the second speaker of the proposition uses a same key term in a slightly different way from the first speaker, because the inconsistency reflects either team incoherence or logical inconsistency on either one of the speakers.

> **Motion**: Women should be given full equality.
>
> If the first speaker defines "equality" as equality of opportunity but not necessarily equality of outcome, but the second speaker talks about how fewer women are occupying the top positions in a company and therefore there is no equality yet, then there is a clear discrepancy in the meaning of the word "equality" between the two speakers. The second speaker is obviously taking issue with the inequality of outcome instead of opportunity, which is not the definition provided by the first speaker.

3

BUILDING A CASE

"I could not fail to disagree with you less."

— BORIS JOHNSON, mayor of London

ONCE YOU HAVE understood what the debate topic is about, how do you go about agreeing or disagreeing with it? Brainstorming for a thousand different arguments for or against the topic is inefficient and almost definitely going to be incoherent. To build a clear case, you have to think about the big picture first – provide an overview of how your team has analysed the issue and how you intend to structure your case to convince the judges and audience. After you have built your case, you will then have a strong framework within which to brainstorm points that are both relevant and useful.

Identify the stakeholders

The topic being debated is usually controversial – otherwise there would be little point in discussing it. And the fact that it has generated so much controversy means that it affects different groups of people in different ways.

There are two broad groups of stakeholders: Those who are affected by a decision, and those who control the outcome.
These are the two most important groups of stakeholders to consider in a debate. There is a third group – bystanders – who may have some opinions about the outcome of the topic, but given the limited time in a debate and the minimal involvement of this group, it's wise to focus on just the first two groups of stakeholders.

Motion: We should remove religion from the classrooms.

Individuals who are *affected* by the outcome: In this motion, if the proposition wins, then obviously all students will be affected by the decision. Students have very little direct influence to determine the outcome of the motion.

Individuals who can control the outcome: The government (via the education ministry) can enforce religion as part of the school curriculum through school regulations; school administrations (via the board of directors, if it is a private school) can also make the decision, if there are no specific laws prohibiting it; parents (who have voting power and thus influence the government's decisions, or can choose to stop sending their children to such schools and thus make an impact through shifting market demand away) are also a strong determining factor; religious leaders and organisations (who are often implicitly very powerful lobby groups) can sway the government decision in some countries.

Bystanders: Other countries' governments may have some

opinions on this issue—especially if there are minorities who are disadvantaged because their religion is not represented in these schools. However, it is highly unlikely that these other governments' opinions can influence the decision in any way, and so they should be classified as part of the bystanders.

What are the motives and incentives for each group?

If you were a lawyer for the prosecution in a court case, you would want to determine if the defendant had a motive to do whatever crime was committed. Similar to having a motive, in a debate each group of stakeholders has its own set of vested interests and incentives. It is important to understand these vested interests in order to analyse how the stakeholders would respond or feel under the new policy being debated.

The theory behind incentives can be found in political science, sociology, economics and literature. Governments are motivated by power (votes); companies by money (profit); and individuals by self-interest (survival and income). Research your stakeholders to find out their incentives and responsibilities.

What are the duties and responsibilities of the stakeholders?

In a court case, the defendant may be found guilty not because of something he did, but because of some responsibility that he failed to perform (often called criminal negligence). Hence, the second thing that we need to understand about each stakeholder is what his or her responsibilities are.

Even if you cannot please everybody in your case, you must show that some parties are happier from your side of the case, and the others are made no worse off (if possible). All debates involve some form of trade-off or compromise; it's unlikely that you'll find a perfect "win-win" solution where all parties are made much better off. Different groups of people have different incentive structures that drive them to act in different ways, and in order to build a case, you need to understand how the people in your case will react to a new proposal.

Motion: We should remove religion from the classrooms.

Continuing the above example, a weak proposition team may claim that schools should teach religion because religious values are "universal and good," and thus the government should enforce this new proposal. This sounds somewhat reasonable on the surface, but a clever opposition can point out that this is incorrect based on a deeper understanding of the incentives of the key stakeholders.

Parents (as key stakeholders) are actually a diverse group and they want what is best for their children — and the diversity of parents necessarily means that there is a broad diversity of views on whether religion-affiliated schools are better for them or not. So if some parents think that religious schools offer a healthier school environment, we should allow parents the option of sending their children to those schools and reject the proposition's proposal. Parents would not be supportive of this government policy that restricts their options and would vote against it. It is not in the interests of parents to restrict their own options.

Understand the motives of stakeholders who can control or influence the outcome.

Understanding their incentives and responsibilities is very important in a debate. An individual is usually motivated to follow the incentive measures for their own *self-interested reasons*. Responsibilities are the burdens placed by their superiors, by the state, or by virtue of their appointment.

Parents are responsible for the upbringing of their children, but some parents, especially those too distracted by their own problems (marital infidelity, financial troubles, legal problems) may have an incentive structure that is out of alignment with their responsibilities. This sometimes leads to tragic consequences (parents who mistreat their children) if specific measures are not put in place. Incentives and responsibilities are not fixed; depending on the context, or depending on whether we are talking about the long-run or short-run, the incentives and responsibilities may change.

Groups that are affected by the outcome are also important, even if they have no power to influence the decision.

There are always some people who are affected by an issue significantly but are unable to change the outcome, because of a lack of influence or voice in the matter. Some teams take this as a sign that the group is thus unimportant to the debate – but this is far from the truth! If a group cannot protect their own interests, then another group (such as the government) should do it for them – this is a key principle of any civilised society.

Motion: We should remove religion from the classrooms.

The secular children who would be forced to learn religion in schools are clearly impacted by the policy, but they are too young to protest meaningfully and are thus "powerless." Does this mean that we should ignore them? No. After all, why should richer nations help poorer ones? Why should we give aid — developmental or monetary — to struggling nations? Why should we ask countries to clean up their treatment of workers and children before we will trade with them? Why should governments consider the rights of the unborn child in an abortion debate? These questions arise in a debate, asking us (or asking somebody with the power to change the outcome) to act in the interests of those who cannot change the outcome themselves.

Structure a case

It is much easier to convince someone if the structure of your case has been thought through well. You are welcome to try the other way, to persuade somebody by rambling for ten minutes, blending between different topic areas, jumping back and forth between unrelated issues. Let me know how that goes for you.

A debate case should have a story-line.

A good story has a beginning, a middle, and an end; the plot leads you from start to finish. That's what a debate case should be like. How do you tell this story, build up the plot step by step, to draw listeners to your side? If you have a team of speakers on your side, how do you spread the case between the various speakers so that it is most convincing? This section explains how to create a story-line that starts well, is coherent and consistent in the middle, and builds up to an exciting conclusion.

The beginning should include the following parts: A definition of the topic, an explanation as to what the "burden of proof" is (that is, what does your team need to prove in order to win), and how your team intends to do this. This is where the previous section, on the key stakeholders, comes in very useful – if you understand who cares about the outcome of the debate, you will understand what the key issues are, and this will be very useful for your case structure.

Your case structure must be intuitive, holistic, non-repetitive.

Cover all the areas that are necessary to prove your case (holistic); make it easy for an audience to follow and understand (intuitive); and do not repeat the same point in different sections (non-repetitive). Here's a good rule-of-thumb: If you find you need to explain lengthily why your case is divided in the way you have decided, or if the case division is not immediately apparent, or if your structure requires you to repeat arguments, then something is not right, and you should reconsider how to split your case.

There is no definitive way of splitting or structuring a case. Normally, your case structure will follow closely from the criteria you have set up to evaluate your side of the case. Here are some other examples (this list is not exhaustive) of how you could structure your case by grouping your points in a logical way:

Ways to structure a case

- By key stakeholders
- By country, or region, or First World/Third World
- By perspective (e.g., macro/micro, society/individual, domestic/international
- By sphere of activity (e.g., political/economic/social/technological/scientific)
- By time-frame (e.g., short-run/long-run)

Decide your structure first, then the order of the points.

It is no good just presenting "a bunch of great points" in random order or even in the order in which you brainstormed them. Present your arguments in a way that fits a *structure*. A certain thematic link should exist between all your points. Once you've got the structure set, then you can think of the order; for instance, if you structure your case temporally, will you discuss the short-run or the long-run first?

The most important points should always be made first.

I know that seems *really* obvious, but you'd be surprised how often people don't do this. Some debate teams think that it is more "egalitarian" to give the most important point to the second speaker so that he or she feels more valuable. Sure, it's egalitarian, but it's also illogical and really bad strategy. The most important point must always come out early. If you begin with a weaker argument, you waste time defending and rebutting this early and weak argument, which will then waste the time of your subsequent speakers, who need to bring out the stronger points.

Even in a non-debate setting, you have very limited time to capture the attention and support of your audience. If you waste the first few minutes talking about less-important points, your audience will lose interest quickly. If you really want to keep your best point for the end, you should state that there is something exciting coming up, so that they know what to expect from your speech as a whole.

Create a case-line

"*Yes, we can.*"

— BARACK OBAMA's campaign slogan

For a strong case, you must be able to articulate your entire strategy in a simple sentence – debaters sometimes call this a catch-phrase, a slogan, a case-line, a tag-line or a base-line (we'll stick to case-line for this section). The case-line is the team's case expressed in one line; it is the simple answer to the question of why the adjudicators and audience should believe that your side is correct. When you say "The motion is true because...," the case-line is the portion that follows the "because."

Example of a case-line: "The motion is true because it is in the best interests of the children and society, and implementing the measures proposed in the motion will eradicate the problem of societal inequality in the long term."

> This is a very simple case-line, and even though I did not tell you the motion anywhere in that quote, you still have a pretty good idea of what the team intends to do and why just from the case-line.

After every major point or argument, repeat the mantra, drum it into the heads of the audience. Your case-line should be broad enough to cover all the big areas of what you intend to prove, and also explain why that directly addresses the motion for the debate. You should also aim for *brevity* in your case-line because nobody like repeating or remembering very long sentences.

The case-line should be memorable and intuitive.
Think of a catchy way to phrase your case-line, but without altering the meaning; try repetition, emphasis, acronyms, humour.

> In one debate I judged, the first speaker of the proposition ended with the line, "Because I have shown you that the people *want it*, and I have shown you why society *needs it*, and my second speaker will elaborate further on why we *can do it*, please go with the proposition." Needless to say, the second speaker ended his speech about feasibility with the line, "As a team, we have shown you that we *want* it, we *need* it, and I have just shown you that we *can do it*. There is no reason at all why the proposition's case should not stand." The repetition worked amazingly well, and even after the debate, I was left with an indelible impression of those impassioned and memorable endings ("We want it! We need it! We can do it!").
>
> Another and more common case-line is identifying the actors in the debate and stating, "We as a team will show you that it is in the best interests of the children, the parents, society, and the responsibility of the government, to enact the ban on...."

Propose a course of action

> *"You teach a child to read, and he or her will be able to pass a literacy test."*
>
> — GEORGE W. BUSH, with his proposal for solving literacy problems

Sometimes, teams are required to provide a somewhat detailed solution to the problem at hand. Airy-fairy wand-waving solutions are not acceptable, such as a silly speaker who states, "… and the *government will fix the problems* associated with gambling such that we will not have any social backlash and thus we are still in favour of legalising gambling." How will the government "fix" gambling problems? Will they use hypnotherapists? Magic? Circus clowns with assault weapons guarding the casinos? Clearly, it is sometimes important to explain how a solution will work.

What is a policy useful for in a debate?

Your *policy* – the debate term for your solution or proposed course of action – must be detailed enough to give people a clear idea of how your solution will work. For your own sake, keep the policy simple and straightforward – long, tortuous clauses and preamble not only waste time, but complicate the debate and make it harder to convince a judge that your solution is workable. Some debate formats require you to detail the legislative changes and mechanisms, while other formats just need you to explain in simple English what your policy does. When in doubt, follow the principle that the simplest solution is the best.

To build your policy, you must establish:

1. That there is a problem in the status quo or as defined in the motion;
2. That a solution is required to achieve certain objectives; and finally
3. What the mechanisms of your policy are – in terms of how the policy will be enacted, enforced, funded – and why this is a reasonable implementation.

The first two points were explained in the previous chapter, so the link between understanding the topic and then building your case is now even more apparent: Without a problem or criteria, you have no idea what your solution is addressing or trying to achieve. The third point, on the mechanisms of the policy, requires some elaboration.

Let's use the example topic, "First-time parents should be made to attend mandatory parenting classes" to show what to cover for the mechanisms of a policy.

What does the policy aim to achieve?

This is the key aspect of the policy – you must give sufficient details of what your policy aims to achieve, so people know what to expect. You should paint a brief picture of what the outcome will look like for the parties concerned.

> What is your objective for having first-time parents attend mandatory parenting classes? Do parents currently lack information on how to raise a baby? What do the classes intend to teach? Nutrition? Biology? Spiritual and moral education?

Who will implement it, why, and how?

You must explain which stakeholders in the debate have an incentive or responsibility to enact your policy. You should also explain how these stakeholders would enact, enforce, and fund your policy, if these are relevant details to the motion.

> Are you proposing that parents must attend weekly parenting classes for the entire duration of the wife's pregnancy? Or is it just a once-off weekend lecture? Will doctors and psychologists conduct it? Religious leaders? Or other parents? Or will the free market be left to determine the best parenting class, but all parents must show evidence of attending at least five hours of classes? Each of these is a very different policy for the same motion.
>
> For this topic, many teams will argue that it is within the government's "duty of care" to take charge of the implementation, because the government must ensure that all children are raised to become good and productive citizens and not criminals or delinquents due to parental neglect. Other teams may state that it is the parents' responsibility to seek a solution, and that the free market could provide one.
>
> Depending on who is implementing it, you will need to address the question of funding as well. Is this going to be fully subsidised by the government? Will poor people be left with lectures from volunteers, while the rich attend fancy classes by overseas professionals? Will it be funded using taxpayer money?

How long will it take for results?

Many teams fall into their own trap of providing a policy and then arguing that the solution will be immediate – this is rarely possible. It is more likely that results will take time, but your policy is a necessary step in the short-run to ensure that your criteria can be achieved in the long-run. You must set the expectations at the start, so that people know exactly when your policy may be expected to produce results.

> For motions where the free market economy is left to find some sort of equilibrium (such as in our parenting classes), it may take a few years before a few clear market leaders emerge, but once they do, your objectives can be achieved. State this upfront so that people know what you are promising—and conversely, what you are not promising.

Why will your policy work?

In a short phrase, you can explain how your policy will achieve your aims, and why you think it is possible to implement it (Do you have the legal or moral authority to enact this policy? Will it work?). Most teams neglect this because it seems so obvious, but that's precisely why you should state it – it is an easy point to score.

Sometimes the principle is only as good as how successfully the policy can be implemented.

Teams must always bear in mind that the ability to implement a proposal is an important precondition to the acceptance of the case as a whole. If a solution is impracticable, there is no point discussing the topic any further.

> **Motion**: We support the death penalty.
>
> The opposition could explain that since it is impossible to prevent innocent people from being hanged (because of numerous factors, e.g., bad lawyers, falsified evidence, legal technicalities), it would be impossible to support the death penalty because innocent people should never be exposed to the risk of being killed by the justice system; thus, even if the proposition can prove that the principle of the death penalty (as a deterrent for potential criminals) is good,

the problems in the practice (and policy) supporting this principle are so flawed that it is better to avoid supporting the death penalty altogether.

Some debate formats do not require a team to propose a policy – but this does not mean you can happily unload the responsibility of explaining that your case is feasible in reality. If you are arguing that we should censor the internet, a logical question that the judge would be asking is, "*Can* we censor the internet with current technology?" I would say that having a well-thought-through policy is very important as it allows you to focus on the real debate at hand: the principles of your case.

"You ask, what is our policy? I say it is to wage war by land, sea, and air. War with all our might and with all the strength that God has given to us, and to wage war against a monstrous tyranny never surpassed in the dark and lamentable catalogue of human crime. That is our policy."

— WINSTON CHURCHILL

4

LOGICAL ARGUMENTS

"Smoking kills. If you're killed, you've lost a very important part of your life."

— BROOKE SHIELDS, making her version of a "logical argument" for an anti-smoking campaign

---

LOGIC IS ANOTHER very important part of our lives, but unfortunately not all people possess the ability to use it (apparently). Debating requires persuasive arguments, and these arguments need to be logical, substantiated, and relevant to the case that your side is putting forward. Strong cases are built with strong, logical, arguments.

Argument structure

Each individual argument needs to have a structure.

We have already discussed how to structure a case. Within your case, there will be a number of different arguments. Each argument needs to be structured in order to coherently and robustly prove your case to the audience.

Argument = Title + Reason + Evidence + Significance.

I always teach my younger students the following mnemonic: When you need to make an argument, don't stress, TRES! An argument that follows this simple structure will always be more robust.

Firstly, each argument has to begin with a *title* that informs people what your argument is going to be about. Next, you should explain the *reason* why the point is logical and rational. You should then substantiate your argument with well-researched *evidence* to prove that it is true. Finally, you must conclude and explain to the audience the *significance* of the point you have just explained, and how it links back to and thus proves your case.

This last step is important because it is wrong to assume that people will automatically understand why you made the argument in the first place. Furthermore, you should always be clear and explicit about what you are proving and why – the audience will not "fill in the blanks" in your case for you.

Every part of the case structure needs to be supported by at least one argument.

In the previous chapter, we looked at how to structure a case in order to prove the motion, and how to divide that case up among the speakers in your team. The case will require a number of arguments to be made – for example, that abolishing smoking is good for our health, good for the environment, and sends the right message from the government to society about unhealthy vices. For each portion of that case, you should have at least one argument. That is, you should have at least one argument to prove that abolishing smoking is good for our health, another separate argument to prove that abolishing smoking is good for the environment, and so on.

Don't go overboard and have too many arguments in your case – not only will you overload the audience, you will probably end up skimming the surface of many points, and not proving anything robustly. It's better to have a few well-crafted and thorough arguments.

Title

Each argument should start with a concise, and relevant title. The title provides an easy reference for you, your opponent, and most importantly, the audience and adjudicator, so that everybody knows what has been established and what needs to be rebutted.

Starting with a title informs the audience and the judges that you are moving on to a new argument. This helps people mentally track and remember your speech, because the titles act like chapter titles for your speech. A good title allows your last speaker to summarise the team's case much more easily, because all they need to do is recount all the argument titles from your side and the other side.

> **Bad example**: "I will now prove the third sub-tier of my major substantives." Or, "Next, the issue of environmental carcinogens." These do not reveal anything about what the argument is about, and are not very accessible at all to an audience. Also, it's likely the audience will not be able to remember what the "third sub-tier" or what the "issue" of environmental carcinogens refers to, if you refer to that label later on in your speech.

Good example: "I will now prove that banning smoking in public places will directly result in a healthier society." This is a clear, concise and relevant title for all to latch on to, and gives the audience a clear indication of what you want to prove.

A good title is a one-sentence conclusion of the argument.
You can think of the title as the *because* that explains why each section of your argument structure is true. State the conclusion of your point in a simple sentence so that the audience knows what to expect and why. It's extremely frustrating for an audience to listen to someone without knowing why this is important. Remember, unlike drama and suspense novels, persuasive speech and debate require you to be clear and direct as far as possible. So unless you have a brilliant reason to depart from this norm, stick to the basics.

Motion: Smoking should be banned.
One possible argument for this motion could be that a ban would send the right message from the government to the people that these vices will not tolerated. A good title for this argument would be: "Banning smoking sends the right message to society that the government does not condone this unhealthy vice."

Reason

"Contrariwise, if it was so, it might be; and if it were so, it would be; but as it isn't, it ain't. That's logic."

— TWEEDLEDEE in Lewis Carroll's *Through the Looking Glass*

As a debater, you must make sense. This sounds simple, but it is often the hardest part, because crafting logical points is something that requires skill, knowledge, and effort – especially when it comes to doing the research.

Proving correlation is not enough; always prove causation.

In daily life, we often mistake *correlation* (when two things are observed to occur simultaneously or sequentially) for *causation* (that the second thing is a direct result and effect of the first thing and not just coincidence) – and many debaters make the same mistake.

As a debater, you must always aim to prove causation, and never stop at merely correlation. In order to prove that one thing is the direct result or effect of the other, you must prove more than the fact that the two things happen together all the time – you must explain *why* there is causation.

> In 1665, Isaac Newton observed apples falling to the ground (or so the story goes). His biographer wrote that Newton wondered why the apple fell to the ground each time — why did it not go up or sideways? He argued that just because an apple fell from the tree to the ground every time did not explain why it fell, nor did it prove that the apple would always continue to fall to the ground in the future. Until he came up with the theory of gravity to explain why there was a causative effect, it was purely correlation.

Theory can help explain why one thing causes another.

You must bridge the causation-correlation divide with some theoretical framework. You must provide a logical explanation to link the evidence together and make it a believable argument. There are a number of ways to prove causation and to establish the reasons for the cause-effect relationship.

Give the most likely and most plausible cause.

Stick to explanations that are aligned with *well-established theory*. Even if you have a great argument to explain why conventional theory is wrong, you are making it unnecessarily difficult for yourself by choosing an explanation that requires so much time and effort to prove. Stick to the commonly agreed theory as the foundation for your reason. "Occam's Razor" (otherwise known as the Law of Parsimony or Simplicity) states that all other things being equal, the simplest explanation or solution is usually the best one. Complex explanations are often wrong – or, at least, are much harder to prove to be correct.

> **Negative example**: "Smoking in public places should not be banned because there is still no real, conclusive proof that second-hand smoke is harmful."
>
> Arguing that smoking does not cause cancer might have been a good argument about twenty years ago, but today you will be mocked if you try to propose this because it defies conventional scientific wisdom. It is a very hard task to convince people of this in your short speech. Pick a more plausible reason and argue for that instead.

Use simple deductive logic to prove your hypothesis.

Deduction is the process by which you come to a conclusion based on a reasonable set of assumptions. There are many in-depth textbooks that explain exactly how deductive logic works, but for the purposes of debate, the basics should suffice:

Deduction: Prove the conclusion by validating each assumption behind it.

In other words, "Hypothesis H must be true if Assumption A is true.

Assumption A can be validated by evidence. Therefore Hypothesis H is most likely true."

Motion: Trade embargoes are more effective than diplomacy on countries with poor human-rights records.
If you want to prove the above motion (that would be your hypothesis), you could argue that countries with poor human rights records are less likely to respond to soft diplomatic pressure than to direct economic pain because they are run by leaders who don't care about global opinion of their actions (assumption). Countries like North Korea and South Africa ignored calls for talks and diplomatic pressure for decades, but once trade embargoes were put in place, the governments felt the economic pain and were forced to open up to talks (evidence). Therefore, the hypothesis that trade embargoes are a more effective solution is true.

Deduction: Get to your conclusion step by step.
Sometimes it is not possible to establish direct "one-step" proof for your claim. In these cases, you must lead the audience along the "process of discovery" to your conclusion. This step-by-step process goes like this: If A then B, if B then C, therefore C is true since A and B are true.

Motion: Euthanasia should be legalised.
To prove that allowing euthanasia maximises limited medical resources — which is a difficult point to establish directly — you can prove it step-by-step thus: Medical resources are limited because there are not enough doctors, nurses and hospital beds in the status quo (as evidenced by long waiting times before surgery or treatment). Medical resources are thus precious and should not be wasted. Therefore, it should only be given to individuals who want it and/or will benefit from treatment. Terminally ill patients who want it can still

be given treatment because they believe they will benefit from treatment, at least psychologically. However, terminally ill patients who do not want it and will not benefit (psychologically or medically) from the treatment are not going to be better off, and giving them the same medical care as other patients who want and need treatment will not be an effective use of the limited resources. Hence, allowing them the option of euthanasia maximises limited medical resources.

Eliminate other conclusions.

This is the reverse of the above process: Only if assumption A is true can hypothesis H be true. Assumption A is not true and this can be validated by evidence. Therefore hypothesis H is most likely false.

General example: If John were a very good friend, he would help you in your time of need. John has not helped you at all in your times of need. Therefore, John is probably not a very good friend.

Motion: The death penalty is ineffective in deterring murderers.
Let's say that your hypothesis was that the death penalty policy is ineffective in deterring murderers. Only if the murder rate were lower in countries with a death penalty would this hypothesis be true (assumption). The evidence and statistics indicate that rates of murder and serious crime in countries with the death penalty are not lower than in countries without the death penalty — therefore we must eliminate the conclusion that the death penalty is effective in deterring murderers.

Eliminating other conclusions: Reductio ad absurdum.

This is a special case of eliminating a conclusion, in which you do so by proving that the *opposite conclusion* is so ridiculous that it cannot possibly be true. This leaves your argument sounding more logical by default.

The ancient Greek philosopher Epicurus argued that the existence of evil in the world is proof that God cannot exist (a very controversial claim indeed). He stated that, in order for God to be a "God" (that is, to have the defining characteristics of a God), God must be omniscient (can see everything), omnipotent (all-powerful and can change anything) and benevolent (have good intentions). However, the fact is that "bad" (evil) exists in the world, as evidenced by crime, disease, and natural disasters. So if God exists, and so does evil, this means that either he does not know about the evil (he is not omniscient), or he cannot stop the evil (he is not omnipotent), or he knows and can stop it but he wants evil things to happen (he is not benevolent). Since we cannot accept any of those possibilities for our notion of God to be consistent (as an omniscient, omnipotent and benevolent being all at once), using the reductio ad absurdum logic, this philosopher concluded that our definition and understanding of God was incorrect (or even that God could not exist).

> *"There are known knowns. These are things we know that we know. There are known unknowns. That is to say, there are things we know we don't know. But, there are also unknown unknowns. These are things we don't know we don't know."*
>
> — DONALD RUMSFELD,
> confusing people with
> what he doesn't know

Eliminating other conclusions: The "slippery slope."

Debaters often use a form of logic referred to as the "slippery slope." This argument explains how certain policies will lead to a long-term undesirable consequence even if the intermediate steps seem fairly benign right now.

> In a debate on allowing euthanasia, one speaker made the badly phrased argument that individuals who are in great psychological and physical suffering should have the right to choose when their life ends (hence arguing that the freedom of choice should extend to the choice to die "with dignity" in this situation). The opposition pounced on this point and said that this may seem like a smart policy for this one situation, but if the government dictates that you are allowed to end your life at your own choosing, then you walk down the slippery slope of legalising all suicide by definition (people have the right to die whenever they choose) — so should suicide be legalised by the government as well? Naturally, the proposition speaker was caught in a dilemma by this trap, and faltered.

Logic is something that has a long philosophical history, and many of the ways to prove causation are extremely complicated. The method you choose to establish causation (the *reason*) should be the simplest method possible – the audience does not have the patience to listen to complicated theoretical frameworks, and you also probably don't have time to ramble on about philosophical logic. In the next chapter on rebuttals, we will discuss how to spot and debunk some common logical fallacies.

Evidence

> *"Well, there is no question that we have evidence and information that Iraq has weapons of mass destruction, biological and chemical particularly."*
>
> — ARI FLEISCHER, White House press secretary, 21 March 2003. No such evidence was found or produced.

An argument is very compelling when you are able to find evidence to support your claim. This evidence can take many forms, and depending on the type of argument you are making, you should select the type of evidence that works best. In this section we'll examine a few different types of evidence that you can use to support your claims.

Use examples and case-studies from real life.

These are real-life case-studies that are used to substantiate a generalised claim in your case. You can find these case studies in newspapers, magazines, or in academic journals (it is better to use academic journals if the theory you are trying to validate is a complex one).

Use more than one example.

Singular examples do not give enough data to validate a claim, and can often be the odd one out (also known as the statistical outlier). Simply put, just because the world's tallest man is Chinese, does it mean that all Chinese are very tall? Do not rely on one isolated example to validate a claim or theory.

Motion: We should legalise prostitution.

If a team tries to argue that legalising prostitution will not cause societal decay because Singapore has done so and is still a moral society, using just the example of Singapore alone will not suffice. This is because it is impossible to make the generalised claim for all countries based on one example. Singapore may be an isolated case where there are unique circumstances or other factors that maintain Singapore's morality, despite having legalised prostitution. However, if you can show that there are other places have legalised prostitution (such as Holland, some states in America, etc.) and also have not experienced societal decay, then your evidence cannot be brushed aside as isolated.

Use a broad range of examples.

In addition to selecting multiple examples, you must ensure that the examples are diverse and broad enough so that they cannot be dismissed easily due to other factors.

Motion: We should legalise prostitution.

Negative example: Prostitution is legal in the Netherlands, Switzerland, and Austria, proving that societal decay is not a consequence of legalising prostitution.

Even though there are three countries listed above, all are liberal European countries, so some people may doubt that it is possible to legalise prostitution in non-European countries effectively. You should select a wider diversity of examples instead.

Positive example: Prostitution is legal in the Netherlands, Austria, Hong Kong, India, Singapore, Nevada...

Don't forget the "black swans."

The story goes that everybody in the world always believed that all swans in the world were white, because people only saw white swans. One day, somebody spotted a black swan, and it totally demolished the established belief that all swans were white. If you are trying to prove a point, make sure you know the "black swans," the strategic counter-examples. Even if you choose to omit the "black swan" examples from your case, you should at least know something about them in case the other team mentions them (you will learn how to rebut examples in the next chapter).

Use statistics the correct way.

Statistics are good, clear, and crisp – they can be very effective evidence. They are essentially a summary of lots of anecdotes and case-studies. It is said that a single story is an anecdote; a thousand stories are a statistic. Most debaters love to use statistics in the form of surveys or polls from magazines and newspapers, and studies from various academic institutions. The guidelines that apply to other forms of evidence in this section also apply to statistics: Do not assume that just because a statistic exists in a magazine, the statistic is enough to prove your point.

> *"Statistics are like bikinis. What they reveal is suggestive, but what they conceal is vital."*
>
> — AARON LEVENSTEIN

Explain your statistics by providing context.

Sometimes people have difficulty imagining the impact of a particular number or statistic until you put it in context for them.

When I was in college, I saw an art project where the artist put the fortunes of various celebrities and businessmen in context. The total net worth of each of the individuals was placed against the GDPs of the world's poorest countries, as well as against how many starving children those amounts could feed for a year. Knowing that Tiger Woods earned US$769m in 2008 is not as shocking as when you discover that that amount could be used to feed almost half a million starving children for a whole year. Context makes your data much more powerful.

Casual stories about your "friends" are not good examples.

Many of us have fallen into this trap, or heard speakers who have made this mistake. They use "colloquial proof," hearsay, stories about their "friends," and other unverifiable stories as evidence. While it may be a useful device to build rapport with the audience (and we will examine this later under style), it is certainly not persuasive if used as evidence.

Motion: We should abolish examinations in schools.

Negative example: "Well, my best friends and I all find that exams are a bad gauge of our ability, therefore exams are a waste of time."

This is not proper evidence — it is not credible, and it is ridiculous to make a generalised claim about all exams in all schools just because you and your friends think it's a dumb idea.

My friends and I think it's a bad idea to use colloquial examples. So there!

Use simple analogies to explain complex theories.

Sometimes complex points are better explained to an audience using analogies rather than just detailed facts and figures. An analogy is when you explain the original concept by comparing it to a similar abstraction or situation in a different context. You should know what conclusion you aim to achieve with your analogy, and then pick a suitable analogy that is similar enough in the key aspects to your original concept. When you expound on the analogy, avoid explaining features of the analogy that are not relevant to your conclusion. Analogies are only useful to a point though; know when to use them, and when to stop.

> The human body is quite different from a car, but for some points, it could be a useful analogy to imagine the human body as a car. Most car-owners take good care of their car by sending it for regular maintenance, sending it to the workshop if something seems to be wrong with it, and making sure that they put the right type of fuel in it. The human body should also be taken care of with the same diligence and care. You should go to the doctor regularly for annual checkups, you should not ignore any ailments in your body, you should eat and drink well, etc. For this limited point, the analogy between the human body and the car is useful. Don't try and extend the metaphor of humans-as-cars any further.

Cite credible and reputable authorities and sources.

If you wish to cite a study or an authority figure to validate your claim, you must name your source and ensure that your source is credible (reputable, believable and informed) and unbiased (does not have any vested interests in ensuring the outcome of the study). If you don't tell your audience those things, your study or authority figure will not be useful evidence for your case.

Your source must be a credible authority in the field.

A reputable source is one that is known to be an expert in that particular field. University professors would be credible authorities for academic material, Nobel laureates for their thoughts on their field, leaders of states for their political commentary, and so on. Two factors determine credibility. First, the source must be an *authority* in that field (so do not quote Britney Spears on national economic policy). And second, the source must be in the right position to make an *informed* assessment; so, for instance, while the Queen of England is certainly a reputable and credible figure in general, her opinion on the latest hip hop music is probably not very well-informed and thus not very useful to cite.

Your source should not have any vested interest in the issue.
There are many studies that are commissioned by companies or governments to "come up" with findings that are agreeable to the company or government. As with all studies, it is possible to manipulate the data or massage the surveys so that the result comes up to something that they wanted in the first place. Thus, it is critical that you find sources that are unbiased – normally academic research institutes that are public funded or funded by endowments tend to be the most reliable because they are not beholden to any organisation.

> **Motion**: This house would legalise alcohol for youths over 12.
>
> If you want to substantiate your claim that drinking French red wine is good for health, even for youths above 12, you should not quote a study by the Wine Drinking Association of French Scientists (I made that group up), because it's fairly obvious what the conclusion is going to be—and thus highly dubious in terms of its accuracy. Pick a source that is more likely to provide unbiased research.

> *"Anyone who conducts an argument by appealing to authority is not using his intelligence; he is just using his memory."*
>
> — LEONARDO DA VINCI

Significance

In the previous steps, you explained what you intended to prove, gave reasons why it was a logical point, and finally, gave evidence to substantiate the point. To conclude the point, you must *link it back* to the bigger picture of your team's case and the motion – and this is known as establishing the proof, or the significance of the point. You should be explicit about how exactly your point fits into your team's case and why it supports (or disproves) the motion. Without this final critical step, all the effort you have put into explaining the point may be completely wasted – the adjudicator is simply unable to see the relevance of the point.

Negative example: "Having substantiated my points, it is clear that the motion must stand." There is no sense of why your point proves the motion, so this is not a good way to explain the significance of your point.

Positive example: "I have shown you that smoking in public places harms society by increasing health problems among non-smokers. The government has a duty to care for its citizens' health, and thus it should ban smoking in public places." This is a much clearer summary of your point and how it supports the case.

5

REBUTTAL

"Winston, if you were my husband, I'd put poison in your coffee."

"Nancy, if you were my wife, I'd drink it."

– WINSTON CHURCHILL to Lady Nancy Astor

WINSTON CHURCHILL WAS able to defuse an insult with a single sentence. Movie scripts often have witty dialogue filled with clever comebacks. Debaters also aim to defuse arguments or defend against attacks on their case – but using logic and evidence, in addition to wit. Rebuttal requires a sharp mind; you must be able to listen, understand, analyse the flaws, and come up with a good response while on your feet. Debaters do not have the luxury of asking for a "time out" to think of a reply. The core goal of rebuttal is to decrease the persuasiveness of the other side's points.

Listening and understanding

> *"I know that you believe you understand what you think I said, but I'm not sure you realise that what you heard is not what I meant."*
>
> — ROBERT McCLOSKEY

There are many different types of listeners, and I'm sure we have come across all of them at some point in our lives. There is the type of listener that Robert McCloskey describes above – these listeners tend to annoy and infuriate because they are so certain that they have heard you correctly (often before you even finish your point) that they refuse to believe anything to the contrary. Aside from being just painful to talk to, they also make very poor debaters. It quickly becomes clear to the judge that this person has not been listening to the arguments that the other team has been making.

Even presidents sometimes don't listen well.

A particularly powerful and instructive example of bad listening happened during the 1992 American presidential debates, in a "town hall" session where members of the public were allowed to ask short questions to the three candidates – George H.W. Bush, Bill Clinton and Ross Perot.

One audience member asked, "How has the national debt personally affected each of your lives? And if it hasn't, how can you honestly find a cure for the economic problems of the common people if you have no experience in what's ailing them?"

Ross Perot proved to the audience that he was a decent listener by answering the question (and the implied questions) head on; he acknowledged that he was rich, but said that the national debt had affected him so much that he was willing to give up the lifestyle of a rich man in order to join the harsh world of politics, so that future generations could enjoy the same opportunities (to be wealthy) that he had had in America. This showed the audience that Ross Perot had heard the question, and answered it as best he could.

Next came George H.W. Bush, who demonstrated how absolutely disastrously things can go if you are a bad listener:

BUSH: Well, I think the national debt affects everybody.

AUDIENCE MEMBER: *You* personally.

BUSH: Obviously it has a lot to do with interest rates —

SIMPSON (the debate moderator): She's saying, "*You* personally."

AUDIENCE MEMBER: *You*, on a personal basis — how has it affected *you*?

SIMPSON: Has it affected you personally?

BUSH: I'm sure it has. I love my grandchildren —

AUDIENCE MEMBER: How?

BUSH: I want to think that they're going to be able to afford an education. I think that that's an important part of being a parent. If the question — maybe I get it wrong. Are you suggesting that if somebody has means, the national debt doesn't affect them?

AUDIENCE MEMBER: What I'm saying is—

BUSH: I'm not sure I get—help me with the question and I'll try to answer it.

AUDIENCE MEMBER: Well, I've had friends that have been laid off from jobs.

BUSH: Yeah.

AUDIENCE MEMBER: I know people who cannot afford to pay the mortgage on their homes, their car payment. I have personal problems with the national debt. But how has it affected you and if you have no experience in it, how can you help us, if you don't know what we're feeling?

SIMPSON: I think she means more the recession—the economic problems today the country faces rather than the deficit.

BUSH: Well, listen, you ought to be in the White House for a day and hear what I hear and see what I see and read the mail I read and touch the people that I touch from time to time. I was in the Lomax A.M.E. Church. It's a black church just outside of Washington, DC. And I read in the bulletin about teenage pregnancies, about the difficulties that families are having to make ends meet. I talk to parents. I mean, you've got to care. Everybody cares if people aren't doing well...

[BUSH finally goes on to actually answer the question.]

That was truly *awful*. If you go over the script again, the audience member and the moderator had to ask the same question *ten times* before Bush came even close to an answer – and he even cut her off when she was trying to re-explain the question to him at one point! Clinton took this moment to shine, and showed off what an amazingly charming and persuasive speaker he could be when he got his chance to answer the question. Needless to say, Bush suffered immensely from this mistake and eventually lost to Clinton. Even if you are not yet running for president, listening well is one of those skills that you need in order to communicate well.

Listen for key arguments and concepts. Record only what is important.

When the other team is speaking, minimise your own chatter. Do not "zone out" and do not get distracted by the audience. *Listen* to what the speaker is saying. Unless you have the memory of a computer, you should write down what the speaker says. Debaters will make their key arguments explicit, so it should be easy to identify them. Key concepts underpin the arguments – they are the logical grounds for the point, and will be important when formulating your rebuttals, as you will see later on. Listening properly does *not* require you to remember every single word or write down verbatim notes of the speech.

Proposition speaker: "We should ban fast food companies from advertising because the government has a duty to discourage people from eating unhealthy junk food."

Opposition team should write down the following:

1. Key Argument: Government should discourage people from eating unhealthy food, by banning fast food companies from advertising.
2. Key Concept: Government should intervene in the eating habits of its citizens.

If you are well-prepared, you will also be able to "listen out" for what the speaker forgot to say.

Listening involves more than just hearing what the speaker *says*; it requires you to listen out for notable omissions – that is, things that the speaker *forgot to say* (e.g., forgetting to provide evidence for a claim). Why is this important? In a debate, each speaker has a very clear role. His job may be to define the terms, or introduce some key ideas, or to prove some level of the case. He may forget to do this – and unless you catch him and point out that he has failed in his responsibilities, even judges may not notice it. Even in a normal conversation, if the other person launches into his argument without defining the terms or making it clear what the problem is, then you should point it out – and fill in the gap – so that you can have a more fruitful discussion and hopefully come to a better outcome. Instead of coming with a blank sheet of paper and furiously copying down every word that your opponents say, you may want to structure a "template" into the key areas that you expect each speaker to cover and fill them in as they start. The more prepared you are before the debate, the less stress you will have once the debate starts.

If you are the first opposition speaker, you would expect the first proposition to give the definitions, perhaps cover a policy (how the solution would be implemented), the team case-line and case division, and one or two big points. You should thus go in prepared to note all those things down from their first propositions's speech and rebut them systematically. If they do not cover an important area (for example, if a silly first proposition forgets to define a key term in the motion), you should point out that they have not thought through the definitions and offer your own definition instead. Likewise, if one of the subsequent speakers forgets to rebut one of your key arguments, you should point this out. If you limit yourself to copying down everything they say, you will only know what they did say, but may not notice what they forgot to say—which is equally important.

Finding and analysing the flaws

It is most logical to attack an opponent's case in this order: (1) Definitions and scope; (2) Team case and major arguments; (3) Specific important points; and finally, only if necessary, (4) Examples.

Notice that the rebuttal of examples and specific points comes last in importance – yet so many students spend the most time on exactly this area. You are always free to re-order the rebuttal, but make it clear which is the most important rebuttal point and which rebuttals are playing a more secondary role. Try to rebut the point that is most "fundamentally wrong" in their case; that is, if there is a central weakness that can pull the carpet out from under their feet (because their whole case rests on that line of logic), then highlight that weakness first. Imagine the other team's case as a house that you are trying to demolish. You should start with the most important areas first, i.e., the house's foundations, rather than waste time attacking parts of the house that do not contribute to its "structure."

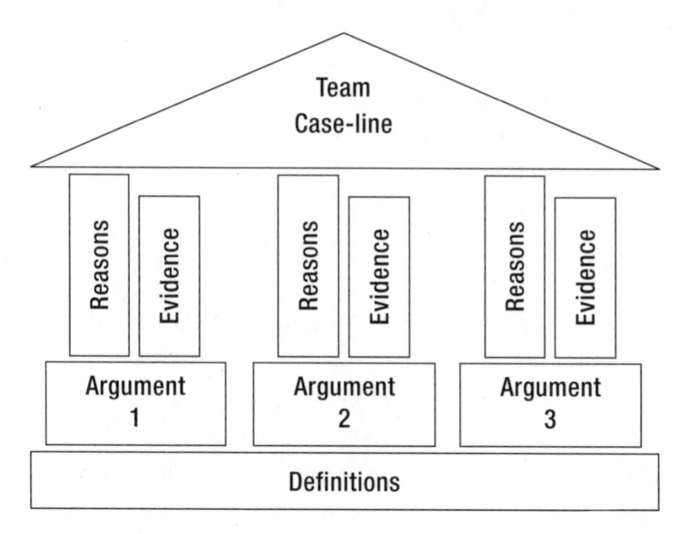

Rebutting definitions

We have already seen in our earlier chapters how definitions can be flawed. If you have ensured that your definition is holistic, well thought-out, fair, and in the spirit of the intended debate, you will find it much easier to bypass or overcome any challenge to your team's definitions.

Once your opening speaker has delivered the definitions, the other team is usually allowed to question some aspects of your definition if they think it is unfair. Your team must be prepared to defend the definitions. If you are on the opposition, you should carefully think about the definitions that have just been presented, and whether they are acceptable and in accordance to what you expected. You may not want to challenge the definition of each term that is different from your definition as an opposition, but you should certainly point out your more significant objections early on.

Definitional debates are messy and should be avoided.

This is a general warning: Judges and audiences dislike when debaters quibble about definitions for too long. They want to see a debate about the topic, not hear both sides disagree about semantics and definitions. You should only disagree with definitions (and therefore start a definitional debate) if you think that it is really, really, *really* important to do so.

Challenge the definition only if the other team's definition is unfair to your case, and only if you have a better alternative.

If the opposing team's definitions are phrased slightly differently from what your side planned, do not assume automatically that you *must* rebut the definition. Some teams object to perfectly fair and legitimate definitions purely because it is not exactly the same as what their team had prepared beforehand – this is unreasonable and quite silly. Ask yourself whether the difference is significant enough to impact your team's case. Will your team's case be disadvantaged if you use their definition? Will your arguments and case be incompatible entirely?

If you agree with the majority of their definition but the phrasing of your definition differs slightly, consider saying that you agree with their definitions broadly, and have some slight *refinements* to offer. This will tell the other team that you are not interested in getting into a lengthy definitional debate.

If you find that the other team has neglected to define a word in the motion that your team considers pivotal to the outcome of the debate, you may *broaden* and *supplement* their definitions.

Determine whether it is better to change your arguments to suit the proposition's definition (if you acknowledge that they have made a fair definition) or whether it is better to challenge the fairness of their definition. Take note: If you challenge their definition and offer an even worse alternative definition (in terms of fairness to both sides of the issue), the adjudicator may look unfavourably upon your team.

Be ready to defend your definition if it's critical to your case.
You must explain the rationale behind your choice of definition, and state why you think it is a fair definition. If (and this is the tricky part) your definition was indeed unfair in some way and the other team has pointed it out, you may want to adopt the "moral high ground" by stating that you think your definition is fair, but in the interest of engaging with their team, you are willing to use both your definition and theirs. It is better to accept the other team's definitions and have a good debate than to bicker about the definition in every round. Adjudicators tend not to penalise a team for accepting the other side's definitions if the team has very good arguments nonetheless. If your case does not depend on the contentious part

of their definition, it is best to move on and avoid a messy definition debate over such a small issue.

If the definition cannot be resolved quickly, you may have to debate using both definitions.

A strategy commonly used is the "even if" argument ("*Even if* we accept their definition to be true, which we do not, their case is still not true because..."). This means that, if you are the opposition, there will be two parallel debates occurring throughout: one on the opposition's "fair" definitions, and one on the proposition's "unfair" definitions (which is the "even if" case). This can get very messy, so you must be clear when your argument is using your own definition, and when the argument is using the other team's definitions.

> The opposition case for a two-definition debate:
>
> "We have proven our case using our own definitions (parallel debate #1).
>
> "We have also explained to you why we think the proposition's definitions A, B, C are unfair and inaccurate. However, they have chosen to keep their definitions. Even if we use their definitions, we can still prove their case is wrong because of the following reasons X, Y, Z (parallel debate #2)."

Rebutting arguments

You must have a rigorous and systematic way of quickly analysing an opponent's case and be able to dissect it within the few minutes you have before your speech. The fastest way to do so is to imagine deconstructing a "logical point" from the previous chapter: First you question the grounds and premise for the *Point* itself, then you question the logic behind the *Reason*, then you dismantle their *Evidence*, and finally, you disprove the *Significance* of their conclusion.

The basic structure for any rebuttal is the same.

Rebuttals normally follow the following basic structure: "They said X. We think X was a weak argument because of these reasons A, B, C. We have told you that actually Y is true because of reasons D, E, F. Therefore, Y is true and it proves our side of the case." In a nutshell, summarise what the opposing team said and explain why it is wrong, then follow up with what your team has said and why it is a stronger argument, and conclude the rebuttal by linking the point back to the motion.

Are the premises of their argument valid?

1. Are there any assertions that cannot be substantiated? Have they made any assumptions about cultural norms, understandings, definitions, etc., that are questionable?

2. Is the context incomplete? Have they failed to present all the facts? Is there something that has been manipulated or suppressed in order to make their claim stand?

3. Have they used a false analogy? In order to use an analogy, it must share sufficient commonality with the actual issue; are there significant differences that invalidate the analogy?

> Many doctors use the analogy of comparing the human body to a car: "If you take good care of your car, it will continue to work; likewise for the human body," they claim. This is false, because one key difference between cars and humans is that cars don't inherit genetic conditions from their parents. This is clearly not the case for humans,

so even proper "care" may not be sufficient to prevent hereditary cancer, for example.

4. Are they guilty of shifting definitions, or equivocation (where they have changed the meaning in order to suit different arguments each time)?

Going back to the example on gender equality, if their first speaker defines equality as "equality of *opportunity* for both sexes" thus implying that open meritocracy is the best system, and their second speaker then claims that the lower number of female students in medical school is proof of inequality, he is not talking about "equality of opportunity," but instead about "equality of *outcome*."

Is the logic and analysis correct?

1. Have they implied that Situation A is caused by a Observation B because they happen at the same time? Just because two things are correlated does not mean that one caused the other – if I poke you today and you win the lottery tomorrow, it is most likely just a coincidence (or I could have magical lottery poking powers).

Some debaters like to make claims like, "Many obese children eat McDonald's (or any fast food, for that matter). Therefore, the growth of McDonald's is responsible for the increasing obesity in children." A good debater can methodically dismantle even a seemingly straightforward claim such as this.

What, then, explains the correlation? (1) Could it be, in fact, that the second thing is the cause of — and not caused by — the first thing (reverse causality)? (2) Could there be a third factor that is causing both the first and second thing? (3) Could there be a complex multicausality at play, such that it is impossible to attribute a single factor alone? Let's consider each of these.

Reverse causality: This may sound odd, but it's possible that the opposite of that claim could be true instead. That is, the increasing number of obese children in the world could actually be causing McDonald's increasing profits, not the other way around. How? McDonald's, like any profit-motivated firm, seeks to produce food that caters to the demand of the consumers in that market segment. If there are many more healthy children who demand for low-fat vegetables, they will seek to produce more vegetables than burgers. However, it is apparent that there are many more obese children who want to eat burgers and therefore do not have any demand for low-fat vegetables. Thus, McDonald's is compelled to produce fattening burgers for their consumers, to cater to market demand.

Third-factor causality: Both the trend of obese children and the trend of McDonald's growing market share could be explained by a third factor. In this case, maybe bad parents are the common reason. Parents who lack dietary control over their kids would allow their kids to have unhealthy lives at home (no exercise, bad diets), and they would also take their fat children to eat more McDonald's (because they don't care about their children's weight). Clearly, good parents would make their child exercise, eat healthily, and avoid too many burgers. So bad parenting is the third factor, or root factor, for both the issues.

Multi-causality: This is a common approach in debates. The world and all the complex interactions within cannot be reduced to such a simple cause-and-effect statement for obesity in children. There are many factors at play in the lives of children: unhealthy lifestyles caused by parents/technology/TV/computer games; bad schooling that does not teach proper nutrition; misleading advertising; parental neglect; Hollywood; etc. The point is, it's not the fault of McDonald's, so don't pin the blame solely on them, because it won't solve the problem.

2. Is the conclusion a *non-sequitur*, unrelated to the factors? Could it merely be coincidence? Is the conclusion completely illogical if taken further?

> Example: Almost all children eat McDonald's, since it is such a pervasive global brand and has strong appeal among that market segment. Does this mean that all children should be obese? If not, then there is something logically wrong with their claim, because the natural conclusion taken further is clearly untrue in the real world. Another variation of this is the claim that "Violent TV causes violent children." Obviously we, and many other children, turned out non-violent despite watching violent TV, so there must be something wrong in that simplistic claim.

3. Is the logic *circular* (does it presuppose the conclusion, or "beg the question")? Circular logic is somewhat difficult to define and identify; sometimes even the person using it is unaware of the fallacy being committed. The initial definition assumes the truth of the conclusion, and the conclusion is proved because of the definition.

> Example: "John is not a liar, because he said he was not." The conclusion clearly depends on whether or not you believe John — he might have been lying when he said he was not a liar!

4. Are they making it into a *loaded issue* or a *loaded question* by including false assumptions into their logic?

> An example of this from a fictitious multiple-choice survey question: "How many times a week do you beat your wife? (a) 1—3 times, (b) 3—7 times, or (c) more than 7 times." This falsely assumes that you have a wife, and that you beat her (because there are no other options).

Is the evidence correct?

1. Are there factual inaccuracies in their argument (authority or study is wrong)? This is clearly the worst error, and most easily rectifiable. Remember to explain the significance of this mistake in terms of the reliability and trustworthiness of the other team's case.

Question the study and the data analysis, provide counter-examples, or otherwise damage the veracity of this facts presented. Are there enough cases and is the study detailed enough to draw such a conclusion? Usually legal cases can be a good source, since you must prove beyond reasonable doubt that your claim is valid. Have plenty of obese children won court cases against McDonald's?

2. Have they failed to summon representative, current, or sufficient examples to make a generalised claim?

> If only a small percentage of children are obese, and only a small subset of these obese children eat McDonald's, then the other team is making a generalised claim derived only from a subset of another subset of cases. This is clearly ridiculous.

3. Are their conclusions based on *colloquial evidence*, i.e., derived purely from personal experience, and not based on researched statistics or data?

> Example: "I met a fat kid the other day who told me he was fat because he ate at McDonald's a lot. Hence, McDonald's is to blame for all the fat kids in the world."

4. Have they given "red herring" examples? These are examples irrelevant to the point being proved, but which can distract or confuse the audience into believing that it is somehow relevant.

In a debate on censorship of nude photography, one speaker might say, "Nude photography is a form of artistic expression and admiration for the human form. Hence it should not be censored." If the opposing speaker said, "We need to prevent the spread of sexual promiscuity by nipping this problem in the bud!" then he or she has misrepresented the point about censorship by shifting the topic to sexual promiscuity (which is the red herring here) instead.

5. Have they created a "straw man" or caricature to rebut, and thus oversimplified or misrepresented the issue? Sometimes, the topic of the debate is shifted to a much broader and harder-to-defend issue.

An example of "straw man" rebuttal in a debate on censorship of nude photography: "If you don't have the courage to stand up against nude photography and censor it, then it is blatantly clear that you enjoy looking at perverse and pornographic images of women who were exploited for their bodies. This is truly worthy of condemnation!" By misrepresenting your position, it is easier to attack.

6. Are they committing "mathematical fallacies" with the evidence, such as incorrect trending?

Example: "I managed to get four As in my exams after studying for a month. I could easily have got eight As if only I had studied for two months." This is a mathematical fallacy that assumes that grades are purely and directly correlated with the amount of time spent studying.

Is their conclusion correct? And even if it is, is it significant?

1. Have they created a *false dichotomy* and presented extreme

options? Are there options that they have not considered that may be more palatable?

> George Bush famously created a false dichotomy when he requested military support from all countries in the "global war on terror" by saying boldly, "You are either with us or against us." Surely there are many other reasons why you would chose not to be "with them" — perhaps you are "with them" in the principle that terrorism should be stopped, but you disagree that a "global war on terror" and an invasion in the Middle East is the best way to achieve these aims.

2. Is their conclusion valid for this particular case, but could lead to a *moral slippery slope* if extended to other cases? If so, then perhaps the broader picture justifies nullifying their conclusion. You must be careful that the slippery slope is logically sound, and not an alarmist or misrepresentative "straw man" point.

> In a debate on teaching secondary school students about safe sex instead of abstinence, the moral slippery slope is that teaching students about safe sex could desensitise them and therefore potentially increase the incidence of underage sex (which is illegal in most parts, yet still prevalent). In the long term, numerous medical problems (more sexual partners increases the risks of receiving sexually transmitted diseases, even if they use condoms) and societal problems (especially in more conservative Asian societies, where parents do not condone premarital sex) could result. Hence a team would be justified in arguing that we should not start down the moral slippery slope of teaching young students safe sex instead of abstinence.

3. *Even if* their conclusion is correct, does it matter to the discussion at hand? Does it change the outcome of the case or the topic? The basic formula of how you would use this rebuttal is thus: "I disagree

with your argument and think it is wrong (for the reasons above). However, *even if it were true*, you are still wrong because..." The (somewhat advanced) example below should clarify how this can be a very powerful tool.

I judged a debate on the topic "We should never negotiate with terrorists," and there was a particularly sharp debater who used the "even if" rebuttals quite effectively. She argued that we should not and cannot negotiate with terrorists. Hypothetically, she argued, in order to try to negotiate with terrorists you need to trust that they will play fair and respond to the normal negotiation incentives as rational people would. However, she argued, terrorists can't be trusted to play fair, because they are not particularly law-abiding gentlemen to begin with, and have no reason to keep up their end of the bargain.

She continued her rebuttal with this: *Even if* you could somehow trust them, you would have to come to a compromise with them — that's part of a negotiation. However, she argued, terrorists have ideological demands that are often impossible to accede to. How, for example, do you appease the terrorist who hates Americans or Jews? Destroy the entire race? Thus, she argued, *even if* you could trust them, you still would not be able to come to a compromise with them.

She then took it one step further: *Even if* you could somehow find a compromise with them for this situation and release the hostages or defuse the bomb, negotiating with terrorists only signals to other terrorists that you are willing to accede to their requests if they use violence, and so you exacerbate the global terrorist problem. So negotiation with terrorists doesn't achieve a good outcome — in fact it achieves the exact opposite because now all terrorists will know that they can force you to negotiate if they start killing innocent people.

This speaker used a series of multiple "even if" rebuttals to disprove the case very effectively, and concluded by saying that all she needed to prove to win her case was that (1) you can't trust them, or (2) that you can't negotiate with them, or (3) that more terrorists would be encouraged by this strategy of negotiation.

Defending your case

Sometimes you need to rebut their rebuttal.

Rebuttal is not always about attacking the other side's case; sometimes you need to use rebuttal to undo damage that the other side has done to your case. Sometimes, you need to rebut *their* rebuttal of *your* case. You need to address the "flaws of your case" that they have pointed out and prove (again) why those criticisms don't stand. That said, even though you are technically defending your case, you should never be on the defensive. You should defend your case, and then go back on the offensive – that's the same advice any military strategist or sports player would give you.

Defend your case in the same priority that you have learned to attack their case.

Assuming that the other speaker has attacked a number of points or arguments in your case, which should you defend first? In our previous section, we discussed which were the more important areas to attack first – that same priority applies here. First, defend attacks on your definition and scope, then attacks on your team case and major arguments, then specific points, and last of all, examples (and only if they are important examples).

To defend, state clearly what the attack was, identify the flaws in it, then explain why it is without merit.
State clearly and directly what the core attack is – you can use the list provided earlier in this chapter to identify what their accusation is. Once you have identified their accusation, you should explain why the accusation does not stand. You can use the rebuttal techniques in this chapter to rebut their accusations. Don't spend too long defending your point – try and be as concise as possible.

Launch your counter-attack quickly.
Once you have defended your argument, you must immediately launch the counter-salvo. Explain that their argument on this issue is actually the one full of flaws instead (and explain the flaws). Moving on to the counter-offensive is an effective and necessary strategy to ensure that the debate focuses on the flaws in *their* case, not yours.

> If the other team accuses your case of being unrealistic because there is no way a government could afford to fund the policy, you can defend it by explaining where your source of funding would come from, and why it is a reasonable amount to pay for such a policy, providing clear reasons and evidence if possible. You should then launch into the counter-offensive by accusing *them* of having an unrealistic policy, preferably on the grounds of funding as well. Make the debate about the weaknesses in their case, rather than putting your own team on a defensive stance.

Preparing rebuttals

Preparing the other side of the case helps you understand where attacks may come from.
Play Devil's Advocate on your own case. Think about what the other

team might say on the motion, and how they might attack your case. If you are so convinced of your own side that you cannot see any opposing arguments, ask somebody to pretend to be the other side so they can poke holes in your case and point out the flaws. Then think how you could rebut the case, the arguments, and even examples that the other side might raise.

Once you have done that, you now have two ways of deploying these prepared rebuttals: (1) Wait until the other team raises the issue (or a similar issue) and then tweak your response accordingly and rebut them, and (2) pre-empt their case and demolish the logic before they have a chance to raise it. There are strengths and dangers in both options.

Make sure your prepared rebuttal is relevant to the debate that actually unfolds.

If you choose to wait until they raise the issue, make sure that your rebuttal addresses directly the point that they raise and not the point that you thought they would raise – the difference does matter, and judges will notice if your team is rebutting points that weren't really raised. The advantage of doing it this way is that you allow the other side to step into your "trap" and then demolish their argument with a well-prepared, concise, logical and substantiated rebuttal.

Use pre-emptive rebuttals sparingly.

Before the other side has a chance to attack your case, you may try stating up-front that you know that there are some flaws in or some critics of the approach your team is proposing – but then you must go on to explain why these flaws are either insignificant, incorrect, or how these critics have been proven wrong. The other team may still pursue the issue, but you have taken out the wind from their sails because you deflated the point before they could raise it. They will now face an uphill battle to win over the judges and audience again. The obvious downsides of this approach are that you may give them ideas that they may not have thought of initially. The judges may also interpret this move as debating against a "make-believe" opposition case, rather than rebutting what the other team has actually presented. Most debaters tend to avoid this approach unless there is a commonly used argument against their case and they wish to destroy this key attack early in the debate.

6

INTERJECTIONS

> *"Yo Taylor, I'm really happy for you, and I'mma let you finish, but Beyonce has one of the best videos of all time."*
>
> — KANYE WEST, interrupting Taylor Swift's acceptance speech at the 2009 Grammy Awards

WE ARE ALL familiar with interjections – they can be something as simple as "Boo!" for a performance we did not enjoy, or "Hear, hear!" when a speaker says something we particularly agree with, or even a harsh insult if you violently disagree with a point that is being made by a speaker. Some formats of debate allow the opposing team to interrupt the speaker with an interjection – in the form of a word, a sentence, or a full argument, depending on the rules. Learning how to handle such interjections in a debate or in common conversation is a vital skill for people who are frequently interviewed, for presenters who get difficult questions from the audience, or for anybody who is put under pressure to come up with good answers to tough questions or comments on the spot. Kanye West proved that his idiotic interjection could derail Taylor Swift. If only she had read this chapter before the Grammy Awards.

What is an interjection

An interjection is a condensed rebuttal in a sentence or two.
An interjection is *not* your chance to start a conversation with the other speaker, or to take over their speaking time. In the American political system, politicians can hijack the debate through an interjection known as a "filibuster" – a sort of verbal weapon of mass destruction that allows them to read out anything (including their grandma's entire cookbook) just to waste time during a debate and thereby paralyse decision-making. This is *not* what intelligent debaters should aim to do (and I find it one of the most ridiculous American political tactics). Debate formats that allow interjections often also place limits on how long your interjection can be, or allow the speaker to cut off your interjection if it gets too long. The lesson from all debate formats – and normal conversations – is the same: Interjections must be crisp. Get to the point of your rebuttal, quickly.

Motion: We should ban school uniforms.

Speaker: "School uniforms are a waste of money—they are expensive, and have no utility outside of school, making them an unnecessary cost to force poor families to endure."

Interjection: "That's incorrect—school uniforms are cheaper than home clothes, and they don't need to be constantly updated to keep up with fashion trends."

An interjection should undermine the persuasiveness of the opposing speaker.

The goal of a debate is to present a more persuasive case than the other team. Interjections help you to reduce the persuasiveness of another speaker by interrupting the flow of the speaker and showing the audience that there are flaws in the argument that they are making. Exposing the flaws as soon as they are made is a more effective way to reduce the persuasiveness of the speaker than waiting till your speech to rebut the arguments.

A good interjection shows you are engaged in the debate.

Another reason interjections are encouraged in competitive debate is that they show the audience and adjudicator that you are constantly listening out for flaws in the speech being made, even when it is not yet your turn to speak (or after your turn has ended). Persuasion consists of more than just the speech you deliver; it is an entire image that you portray and present. If you are confident when you speak, but once you sit down you look terribly nervous and refuse to engage the other speakers, judges may interpret this negatively — and start to doubt whether the speech you delivered was really as persuasive as they thought. Stay engaged in the debate throughout.

Interjections are strategic tools — use them sparingly.

Do not use interjections to harass the speaker, by constantly nagging them or offering them in a menacing way. Do not bombard the speaker with multiple repetitive interjections if it is clear that they are not ready or willing to accept them at that point in their speech. Use them sparingly and intelligently; if you misuse the tool, judges may see it as a sign of an overly aggressive debater, and that is not very persuasive either.

Offering an interjection

Use the rebuttal framework to analyse the flaws in the argument being made by the speaker.

The speaker will most likely be following a similar Point-Reason-Evidence-Significance structure to their own argument, even if they re-order it slightly. Ask yourself the questions from the rebuttal chapter, and analyse the flaws quickly. Crystalise your objection into the key counter-argument you want to make. Rebut the reason, evidence or significance of the point in your interjection.

Zoom in on a single flaw.

If you see multiple problems with the argument being made, pick the most fatal flaw – the underlying logic is usually a good bet – and attack just that. Do not try and attack more than one area with a single interjection. If there is a mistake in their reasoning, point out the logical flaw. If their evidence is wrong or not sufficient to prove their point, explain the mistake. If the point is irrelevant to the motion and not significant, explain why. To use a military metaphor, interjections are best used as surgical strikes, rather than as broad cluster-bombing of many areas.

Make a statement, then follow up with a tough question.

A good way to phrase an interjection is as a "statement then question." Make a counter-point or provide some counter-evidence, then ask the speaker a tough question that links your interjection to the case that was being made. This is quite effective, because it disrupts the flow of the speaker, by forcing them to respond to your question, and also gives you the chance to put the speaker in a tight corner and undermine his persuasiveness.

Motion: We should ban school uniforms.

Speaker: "School uniforms are a waste of money — they are expensive, and have no utility outside of school, making them an unnecessary cost for poor families to endure."

Interjection: "School uniforms are cheaper than multiple sets of home clothes, and don't change with seasonal fashion trends. How can you still claim that school uniforms are a waste of money when the alternative you propose is worse?"

Advanced debaters use interjections to entrap the speaker.

If you are able to foresee a potential flaw in an opposing speaker's case, you can put them in the spot by asking them a question, and later using that answer against them when you get up to speak. (This is very advanced and I would not recommend it for junior debaters.)

Motion: We should ban school uniforms.

Proposition speaker: "School uniforms are a waste of money — they are expensive, and have no utility outside of school, making them an unnecessary cost for poor families to endure."

Interjection: "So your team would support the option that best helps poor families, is that correct?"

Proposition: "Of course! Moving on to my next point."

Later, the opposition speaker can recall the interjection: "I asked him earlier if he wanted to help poor families, and he replied 'Of course.' And yet we see them proposing a more expensive option, an option that forces poor students to either waste money keeping up with fashion trends, or ignore the fashionable clothes and be stigmatised for being poor and not wearing the coolest clothes. The proposition is not helping poor families by banning school uniforms. They are forcing them to either be poorer, or be stigmatised and ridiculed. My team is the one that is helping the poor families."

Responding to an interjection

Now that you know what the goal of an interjection is – to reduce the speaker's persuasiveness – how should you respond when *you* are offered an interjection during your own speech?

If you decide to accept the interjection, listen carefully to it.

Once you have made the decision to accept an interjection and you have informed the other person that you are ready, signal to the audience and adjudicators that you are eager to hear what he has to say. Stop, listen to him, and (if possible) look at him. If the speaker does not make his point quickly, you are allowed to politely cut him off. You should wait until the speaker has ended the key phrase that describes his objection, which normally takes a sentence or two. Do not cut him off before that, because it may appear as though you are unwilling to listen to his point. If the interjector begins to ramble on or repeat himself, you can politely stop him by stating that you are ready to answer his question.

When replying to the interjection, turn and *address the audience and the adjudicator* – you should not face the interjector when giving your response – because the goal is to persuade the audience and adjudicator, not the other speaker.

Listen for the key words in the interjection.

The key words in an interjection will tell you what the interjection is really asking. If the interjection contains a question, then take note of the way the question is phrased. Is it a question of how, where, why, or when? Next, take note of the subjective or contentious word in the interjection, which is the crux of their point.

> Interjection: "How can you claim that your proposal is a better use of money than our proposal?"

Key words: "How" and "better."

The speaker is asking, "How do you determine what is a better use of money?" Or, in other words, "By what standards or criteria do you evaluate which proposal makes the best use of money?"

Once you have broken down the question into a simpler and more accurate question, you can answer it directly and confidently.

If the interjection is questioning the credibility of your examples, respond by citing the source of the examples or providing other examples to show it's not an isolated case.

If the interjection raises doubts about the logic of your point, go step-by-step and show how no causal links have been neglected, and explain why the logic is sound.

If the interjection is just a red herring, tell the audience why it's irrelevant to the motion.

To buy time or to defuse a negative tone, paraphrase.

Vocalise the thought process above – explain what the interjection is really asking, and let the audience know that you understood the question. Phrase the question in such a way that it is more relevant to the debate, and more aligned with your own case. If you get an extremely negative or difficult question, don't go on the defensive; rephrase it to remove the negativity or at least neutralise the sting, and then answer it.

Interjection: "Your policy would waste millions of dollars of precious resources that we should be spending on more worthwhile causes like fighting AIDS!"

Response: "You are asking us to justify whether the money we are proposing to spend on this policy will be well-spent, and whether we can justify the importance of our policy when there are other pressing needs. We can do both. Let me tackle them one by one..."

Respond to the issue of the interjection directly.

Once you have identified the issue and defused the negativity, respond directly to the heart of the issue. The content of your answer should be kept crisp and specific to the issue that you have identified in the previous paragraphs.

Do not end on a defensive note; launch a counterattack.

Once you have answered the interjection, use the chance to drive home your own case again. Don't meekly go back to your case with no smooth segue ("Now that I have responded to their question, let me go back to my case..."). Put the other team on the defensive by launching into a sales pitch about how your case is clearly stronger on that issue they just raised and how they actually should answer a question about the merits of their own policy or case. Always put the other team on the defensive by forcing them to defend their case. Link your response back to the strength of your team's case, and how your response has further strengthened your position.

> Response to interjection, continued: "I have shown you how our policy has a careful system of checks and balances to ensure that the money is well-spent. My previous speaker also showed you that the goals of our policy are important to society — comparable even to finding a cure for some diseases. But what has the other team shown you? Have they shown you how their policy will prevent wastage of money? No. Have they shown you why their goals are important? No. Their case has not robustly answered the important questions, and I challenge them to do so in their next speaker. Until they are able to do this, their policy will not meet the needs of the debate topic today."

STYLE

"I didn't say she stole my wallet."

I OFTEN AMAZE and amuse very young debaters with a "vocal magic trick": I tell them that I will change the meaning of a seven-word sentence seven times to mean seven completely different things, without changing a single word – just by the power of my voice alone. I repeat the sentence above seven times, but each time I put the emphasis on a different word:

> **I** didn't say she stole my wallet (someone else said so).
> I **didn't** say she stole my wallet (emphatic denial).
> I didn't **say** she stole my wallet (I blogged it).
> I didn't say **she** stole my wallet (maybe you did it?).

… and so on. The spoken word is so much more powerful than

the written word because we can add emphasis and emotion and entirely change the meaning of a written speech. Half of all communication happens non-verbally (that is, how you present the words is as important as the words themselves), so learning to communicate and persuade requires you to do much more than compose clever speeches.

Visual style

Visual style is about how you look when you speak.

I often ask my students to watch videos of famous non-English-speaking orators. Adolf Hitler is a terribly powerful example: Just by watching his body language and facial expressions, even people who do not understand German can see that he is a very angry, dominating, and powerful speaker. I also make them watch speeches of famous speakers with the sound turned off. Again, just from looking at the way the speech is delivered, they can see how persuasive the message will be. Barack Obama's posture, hand gestures, and face, for example, ooze credibility and charm. The importance of presenting the argument well should never be underestimated. In fact most books that deal with persuasion focus largely on how to *appear* confident – but those books unfortunately fail to teach the reader how to craft persuasive arguments.

First impressions matter.

As you approach the microphone or stage, the audience is already beginning to assess you. Are you appropriately dressed for the occasion? If you are addressing distinguished senior academics for your thesis presentation or businessmen for a lecture, you might want to wear a suit. If you are addressing an audience of teenagers on the importance of safe sex, perhaps dressing like a boring old nerd is not your best option. In debate competitions, it is best to be dressed in formal school uniform.

Once you get to the microphone, get yourself ready to speak. Set your speech notes properly, adjust the microphone height, take a deep breath, make eye contact with the audience, and get yourself mentally ready to deliver a confident speech. Make the first impression a good one.

Your posture reveals your confidence.

Stand straight. Slouching is not only bad for your spine, it is bad for your persuasiveness. People interpret slouching as a sign of either laziness or lack of confidence – and neither of those traits wins over people's trust.

Move your body only when it is necessary to make a point.

Don't sway from side to side, or rock by shifting your body weight from your heels to your toes. A speaker who rocks, sways, or otherwise dances around the stage unconsciously distracts audiences – and anytime an audience or a judge gets distracted, it means you are losing the "persuasion battle." Stand with both feet firmly planted on the ground.

Use the stage space intelligently.

Some speakers like to stand behind the lectern or podium. Some like to have a microphone stand placed in the middle of the stage. Some like to hold a microphone so they can walk and talk. The choice is yours. I personally think that standing behind a lectern or podium makes it hard for people to read your body language and "absorb" the non-verbal signals that your body is sending them, thus making you less persuasive. That said, many charismatic speakers and politicians have learned how to speak effectively from behind a podium. Speakers who prefer to walk and talk with a microphone in hand must also use their pacing around effectively; pacing around for no reason distracts the adjudicator.

Use gestures sparingly, deliberately and meaningfully.

Some speakers use hand gestures so excessively that it looks comical. They poke the air at every word they say, or they chop some imaginary block after every sentence. Gestures should be selectively used to emphasise specific points or messages. When there is a word that can be illustrated easily with your hands ("just a tiny bit" – make a pinching motion with your fingers; "lots and lots" – arms wider and wider apart; "split apart" – chop something in half, etc.), use a hand gesture. Use hand gestures to visualise words, concepts, numbers, comparisons, to illustrate a sense of scale, or to point at specific things. Remember this though: Debate is not a pantomime. You are not trying to convert your speech into a homemade sign language. Use gestures sparingly.

Other simple movements, like shrugs, winks, nods, and so on, are also useful non-verbal signals to an audience when used sparingly.

If you don't have any specific gesture to make with your hands, just keep them relaxed by your sides. Don't put your hands in your pockets (it's too casual), don't fold your arms, and don't adopt the "praying mantis" or "Tyrannosaurus Rex" arm position (imagine someone with their elbows tucked in to their sides and hands thrust out like tiny T-Rex claws).

Experienced speakers have a very natural flow to their hand gestures that supports their message, but if you find that you are unsure of what to do with your hands, just keep them relaxed by your side so they don't distract the audience.

Make good eye contact with the judges and audience.

Eye contact does wonders. When a speaker looks you in the eye and says something, you feel like that message is directed at you and you alone, and it's very persuasive. Don't stare at your notes or the podium – inanimate objects won't be persuaded no matter how much eye contact you make with them. Reading from your script is the fastest way to lose the attention of your audience. Don't do it.

Making good eye contact is not the same as glancing around a room, or staring directly at an imaginary spot at the back of the room (this is a common tip, but a terrible one, because the audience can tell immediately that you are uncomfortable making eye contact). Making good eye contact is also not about staring at the adjudicators; it's about speaking to them as though you were having a conversation with them.

The focus of the audience's attention should be on your face and eyes – the rest of your body movements, your clothes, and your "accessories" should not distract them from making eye contact with you.

Be in control of your accessories – use a small notebook or index cards for your speech if you are not using a lectern.

If you write your points on loose sheets of paper, you will have difficulty holding them while speaking. Loose sheets of paper are also prone to falling off tables or getting blown away, and you will waste precious minutes trying to pick them back up and sort them out – and quickly lose credibility because of your unprofessionalism.

Some coaches advise their debaters to use small index cards; others swear by small notebooks. Both have their pros and cons, but as long as the item is unobtrusive and easy to handle (and won't fall apart on stage with your shivering fingers), it should serve its purpose well. But if these "speech accessories" are a distraction to the audience, you will find that making eye contact is difficult because they will be watching your notes instead of your eyes.

Vocal style

Vocal style is about how you say it.

The 1960 American presidential-candidate debates between Nixon and Kennedy was the first time that the public could watch the debate on TV instead of just listening to it on radio. On TV, Kennedy came across confident, well-groomed and perfectly tanned, while Nixon, who was recuperating from a two-week stay in hospital, looked tired and dishevelled. Those who watched the debate on television thought that Kennedy clearly won that debate. Interestingly though, those who only heard the radio broadcast thought that Nixon won – his vocal style and arguments were deemed to be superior to Kennedy's. In the previous section, we discussed how it was possible to determine how persuasive a speaker was just by watching the video with no sound. In this section, we will discuss the opposite: Sometimes the *way* a person speaks can persuade an audience.

Speak loud enough to be heard, but don't yell.

If you have a great argument to make, it helps if people can actually hear you. However, audiences baulk at a speaker who yells at them like a drill sergeant. When you walk into the debate venue, look around and determine what volume you will need to speak at to get your message heard by all the audience members – sometimes a small classroom packed with students just needs normal conversation volume. If there is a microphone on the stage, be sure to test it to check that your natural volume is picked up and amplified to the correct level for the auditorium.

Control your speed.

Most people speak at about 120 words per minute. Some people speak a little faster, some a little slower – but if you are trying to cram a few hundred words into that minute, you can be sure that people aren't going to be able to process what you are saying. Debating is not about getting the most arguments out in a limited time; it's about getting the most *persuasive* arguments out in a limited time, and persuasion requires the audience to be able to hear, absorb, and assimilate the words that are coming out of your mouth.

I know that there are some formats of debate that encourage speakers to do what is known affectionately as "the dump," where a speaker tries to overwhelm his opponent by spewing out the most number of factual points or arguments as quickly as possible. This is not easy to listen to, and it is certainly not very persuasive. No great American president ever won an electoral debate by "dumping" on the audience, so I see no reason why this is considered an effective technique.

Your tone and timbre are innate, but a commanding vocal presence can be cultivated.

I once had a classmate who had a naturally squeaky and high-pitched voice, one that most people would not find "commanding," but she trained herself to speak slower and in a slightly lower tone, and over time developed a speaking voice that was much more credible.

Your voice is like a musical instrument (ask any singer) and it can be tuned and trained to take on different sounds. Not everybody can or should try and speak with a natural deep baritone – which has been shown to have the most commanding vocal presence – but if your natural voice is not suitable, develop a "stage voice" which is easier on the audience. One simple method is to sing your favourite songs in a lower key than you normally would sing in. Over time, you will expand the range of your voice and be able to speak comfortably in a deeper voice.

Vary your tone, volume, and speed in order to differentiate important parts of your speech from the rest.

Monotonous speakers are terribly boring to listen to and they can make even the most compelling arguments seem dull, lifeless, and tragically unconvincing. An animated and energetic speaker who uses variation effectively is able to enthuse the crowd and make even the most mundane message seem exciting. Don't get too gimmicky or over-dramatic, but inject some life into your speech to keep the audience interested.

Learn to use a microphone properly.

Different microphones capture your voice differently. Most stage microphones are uni-directional, which means that they respond best if you speak directly into the top. If you have a high-pitched voice, you may want to speak into the bass-sensitive parts of the mic – usually the sides of the microphone dome. Hold the microphone close to your mouth, within an inch of your lips, and below your face. Do not block your face with the microphone. If you are using a microphone stand, adjust the stand such that the microphone is below your face, pointing upward to your lips. Test the microphone before the debate starts, not when you are about to give your speech.

Most importantly, diction, diction, diction.

Pronounce your words clearly and crisply. People tend to speak quite quickly in conversations with friends, and sometimes people speed up when they are on stage, because of nervousness or time pressure. However, the audience may miss some words if you speak too quickly. It would be a tragedy if your brilliant argument was completely ignored because you spoke too quickly and nobody could catch it.

Verbal style

Verbal style is about the words you choose.
True orators know the importance of selecting the right words. A well-crafted case-line is catchy and memorable, and thus ingrained into the audience's memory.

Clear, simple language is better than fancy phrases, jargon.
Debaters are often well-read and typically have a good command of English. Unfortunately, many debaters sometimes get a little carried away with their knowledge of obscure words and (deliberately or inadvertently) slip in a few fancy words instead of using more common terms. Many of us know what a "lacuna" is, but why not just say "gap"? Try and stick to words that the average man on the street knows. This may be difficult to calibrate perfectly (how can you ever know whether the average man on the street will know what "lacuna" means?), but generally speaking, if there is a simpler word, use it. Communication is about being understood by the audience, not about impressing them with your vocabulary.

Be concise; avoid meaningless "verbal fillers."
"Verbal fillers" are meaningless snippets that your brain inserts into the pauses in your speech by accident. Young debaters pepper their speeches with phrases like "Ladies and Gentlemen" or "members of the audience," but these don't add much value or meaning to their message. Other more annoying fillers include the words "like" and "actually." I once judged a debater who spoke like a sitcom character: "Like, so actually, there isn't like a real problem." If the word does not add meaning to the sentence, omit it.

Verbal qualifiers are a slightly different and more troubling issue. Some speakers have developed a habit of including phrases like "I think" and "I guess" in their sentences. These indicate a lack of confidence. You sound tentative and uncertain to the audience, which is again not very persuasive. Obviously if you are speaking, then the point you are making is what *you* think and there is no point re-stating, "*I think* that the death penalty is wrong." Just say, "The death penalty is wrong because..." The qualifiers also indicate a lack of certainty in your arguments. Why do you "guess"? Shouldn't you have researched it and thus "know"?

Qualifiers like "Ok?" and "Right?" added to the end of every sentence also make the debater sound unsure of himself, like he is seeking affirmation or confirmation that he is, in fact, right. As a debater, you should be persuading us that you are right, not asking the audience whether you are right or not.

Add some flourish with repetition, alliteration, quotes, metaphors, and similes.

Advanced speakers should experiment with rhetorical devices that make speeches more memorable. Read famous historical speeches and see how they use words to capture the imaginations of the audience. Martin Luther King, Jr. used repetition famously in his 1963 speech, "I have a dream," and it still resonates in people's minds today. Barack Obama used repetition in his speech at New Hampshire in the run-up to the 2009 elections:

> "For when we have faced down impossible odds, when we've been told we're not ready or that we shouldn't try or that we can't, generations of Americans have responded with a simple creed that sums up the spirit of a people: Yes, we can. Yes, we can. Yes, we can.
>
> "It was a creed written into the founding documents that declared the destiny of a nation: Yes, we can.
>
> "It was whispered by slaves and abolitionists as they blazed a trail towards freedom through the darkest of nights: Yes, we can.
>
> "It was sung by immigrants as they struck out from distant shores

and pioneers who pushed westward against an unforgiving wilderness: Yes, we can.

"It was the call of workers who organised, women who reached for the ballot, a president who chose the moon as our new frontier, and a king who took us to the mountaintop and pointed the way to the promised land: Yes, we can, to justice and equality. Yes, we can, to opportunity and prosperity. Yes, we can heal this nation. Yes, we can repair this world. Yes, we can."

Personal style

Record yourself so you know how you look and sound.

Most people are unaware of their "natural" speaking habits, because many of these habits are subconscious. If you have ever heard a recording of your own voice, you have probably thought to yourself, "Is that really what I look and sound like when I speak?" I strongly recommend that you take a camera and record yourself delivering a full speech from start to finish (either at a debate training, or just by yourself at home). I appeared on a televised debate show a few years ago, and the first time I saw myself on television, I thought, "Why am I always frowning at everybody?" After over ten years of debating, I was still surprised to see what I looked like on video.

If you can, get your debate teammates or friends to watch the video of you giving a speech, and ask them to point out any flaws or areas for improvement. Be critical of yourself. Self-awareness of your mistakes is the first step towards correcting them.

Improve your style by learning from others.

Once you know what your personal style is, and where your areas for improvement are, you can start work on improving your style. The easiest way to do this is through mimicry. Watch videos of better debaters and famous speakers, and try and copy what you see. Learn to incorporate the best parts of many speakers into your own style and practise, practise, practise. Changing personal speech styles takes a lot of time and effort.

Overcome nervousness by focusing on your message, not your situation.

If you are terrified at the thought of standing in front of an audience for six minutes and talking, you are not alone. Many people are afraid of public speaking because they focus on the potential awkwardness of the situation. Avoid that. Focus instead on the message and arguments that you want to deliver. Tell yourself that you have only six minutes to persuade the audience of your very important arguments, so you should quickly get on with your task.

Many debaters get so nervous that they forget to eat or drink before the debate. This is dangerous, and will leave you weaker and dehydrated when you speak. Eat normally if you can, or at least snack before the debate. Have some room-temperature water to drink before you speak (but not too much – you can't run off to the restroom in the middle of a speech).

Memorise your first few sentences.

Most speakers go blank when they step out in front of the audience. One easy way to avoid this danger is to be absolutely certain how to start your speech. Mentally rehearse your opening lines before you get out of your seat. As soon as you get out of your seat, walk purposefully to the microphone or podium, make eye contact with the audience, and deliver those lines exactly as you memorised and rehearsed them. Once you have broken through this "mental block" of the first few sentences, you will find it easier to continue with the rest of your speech.

Most importantly, be confident that you will succeed.
Visualise yourself as a successful and confident debater – what do you look like on stage, winning over audiences with your logic and charm? Keep that picture firmly in your head as the end-goal of your training. Before each debate, visualise yourself going up and delivering your speech confidently. Air Force pilots have a technique called "mental flying," where they imagine themselves getting into the aircraft, starting up and taking off, and performing the mission before coming back for a safe landing. They visualise every detail – what switches to press, how to move the control column, what the instruments and map would look like at each stage. Once they get into the aircraft for real, it feels almost like they've done it before, and thus it reduces the stress of the flight. Debaters should similarly "mental fly" (or is it "mental debate"?), by rehearsing the entire process of going up onto stage, arranging your notes, adjusting the mic, and delivering the speech confidently. When it comes time to do the actual debate speech, you will feel that same sense of confidence that pilots have, knowing that you have already gone through this once in your imagination.

Winning over the audience

Most books only talk about persuading the audience, and break it down to the terms above: visual, verbal, vocal techniques. While that may be good enough to persuade an audience, you may want to go further and capture their imaginations. A speaker who can win over the hearts and minds of an audience is an extraordinary debater.

Start strong. Introductions matter.
Openings grab attention, so start with an interesting and relevant introduction to capture the ears of the audience. You only have one

shot at building rapport with the audience from the start, so make sure your introduction is well-rehearsed and delivered perfectly. There are many ways to start your speech:

- *Quote or literary extract*: A famous and thought-provoking historical or literary perspective on the issue.
- *Statistic or news item*: A surprising or shocking piece of data that jolts the audience.
- *Question or prediction*: A thought-provoking and emotionally powerful rhetorical question or prediction.
- *Anecdote or personal story*: Open up to the audience and explain how this issue is of personal importance to you, and they will warm up to the rest of your points more easily.
- *Joke*: Entertain the audience and break the tension of the debate to win them over.

Try not to start your speech with "I will outline three key points in my speech." Audiences and adjudicators may appreciate the clarity of your structure, but they certainly won't be excited or entertained. Start with a proper introduction, even if it is just a short one. Grab people's attention and make them care about what you have to say.

Be earnest.

An audience can sense when you truly believe the words that are coming out of your mouth, and when you are just speaking vigorously for a topic. Find an angle that you can personally connect with, even if it is not directly relevant to your life. Use that angle and connect with your side of the topic emotionally, and charge yourself up to speak with passion and conviction. Show the audience that the topic matters to you and, by extension, should matter to them. Create emotional resonance, and you can capture their hearts.

> If you are debating about poverty in the Third World, for example, tell the audience about your travels in that region and they impacted you. You may want to ask them a rhetorical question about how they would feel if they had been born in a Third World country. Make them feel connected to the topic in an authentic way.

But don't be a drama queen. If you fake the emotional connection and the audience detects even the slightest bit of falsehood, you will instantly lose their trust – and once you do, you will find it near impossible to win them back.

Be intellectually humble.

Don't brag or boast or use terms that you know are outside the vocabularies of most people. If the topic is complex and required lots of research for you to grasp, say so and explain to the audience how you finally understood the topic. They will be grateful for the explanation, and they will also connect with you as "one of them" – a person who is intelligent enough to understand something but may need a little bit of patience in the explanation. If you speak as though gene-splicing and data-mining are common sense, the layman audience may get alienated from you and side with the other team emotionally.

Be personal.

Connect to the audience. Share a little bit about yourself with them, and they will open up to you. Share an inside joke with them on the topic, or slip in an example or anecdote (a positive one) from the audience's hometown or school – especially powerful if you are at a debate competition that is not at your home ground. Establish rapport with them and show them that you are the one who is on *their* side.

Be polite.

Rude debaters don't win audiences. When you reject interjections, do so politely. When you refer to the illogical arguments of the other team, don't call the speakers half-wits or complain that they haven't been paying attention to your intricate argument – it's quite likely that the audience was not paying attention to the intricacies either. Be polite to the other team, even when they are rude. And don't complain about them during your speech. Nobody likes a whiner.

Be funny.

Witty retorts that come at the expense of the other speaker may generate a few uncomfortable laughs, but it won't endear you to them. Learn how to make witty retorts and comebacks without insulting anybody – even if it means having to insult yourself. Sometimes the best way to get a laugh is with self-deprecating humour; it cannot possibly offend anybody else because the target of the joke is yourself. Some debaters prepare jokes in advance: witty retorts, funny introductions or conclusions for different topic areas, and so on. It's not as spontaneous, but everybody has to start somewhere – not all of us are born comedians.

Humour is one of the best but unfortunately underrated weapons in the debater's arsenal. Humour is difficult to teach, however, because it requires a combination of a sharp and witty mind, good comic timing, and great delivery. Don't try too hard if you're not naturally funny; but if you think you've got it in you, let the inner comedian come out once in a while during the debate.

Be charming.

Don't speak as though you are at the pulpit admonishing sinners. Don't speak as though you are a military general talking to soldiers who have no choice but to sit there and listen to you. Talk to them as though you are in earnest conversation with somebody who is a little sceptical, and you want to ensure that they understand your message before they get up and walk out. Don't take their attention span for granted and bore them to death; keep them interested, keep them captivated. Most importantly, learn to read the audience's faces. If they start looking bored, reignite their interest. If they look lost or confused, explain it again more simply. If they look like they get it and are getting tired of listening to this point, move on. Think of your debate speech as a *conversation* with the audience, not a lecture.

Be inspirational.

Give the audience a vision of your world, of your policy, and show them that this is the dream worth striving for. Make them care about your speech and your objective. Don't be defeatist and whine or complain about how difficult things are. Tell them that your proposal is the *right* thing to do, and that it *can* be done. Inspire them with your vision and they will reward you with their vote.

Be memorable. End strong.

Debate speeches are usually fixed in duration, and there is a timekeeper or chairperson who ensures that you don't speak too long past your allotted time. When the time comes for you to end your speech (usually the timekeeper will signal using a bell of some sort when your time is up), don't just sit down. Conclude your speech properly to give the audience a sense of closure to what you have said in the last few minutes.

Many good speakers end their speech using one of the same tools available for introductions (quotes, facts, anecdotes, etc.). Some speakers are able to condense their entire speech into a memorable soundbite – a single sentence or phrase that captures the essential messages you want the audience to remember. It helps if your case-line itself is very memorable, which would allow you to end using your case-line as a conclusion. Explain to the audience what's in it for them: Why should they care about your case and your speech, and how will it impact their lives?

Another technique is to refer back to your own introduction (or perhaps another speaker's introduction) and "close the loop." This serves to explain how your case answers the question/dilemma/news story that was raised in the introduction. Many famous speakers do this – they raise an issue or a quote at the start of their speech, and repeat the quote at the end, this time emphasising how their speech lived up to the ideals of the quote, or solved the problem raised by the quote at the start.

8

PUTTING IT ALL TOGETHER

"I feel a recipe is only a theme, which an intelligent cook can play each time with a variation."

— MADAME BENOIT,
Canadian cook and author

THIS BOOK IS very similar to a cookbook – we have explored each of the ingredients for a good debate in detail, and now we will attempt to put it all together using the recipes in the earlier chapters. Just like any good recipe, everything in this book can and should be tweaked and experimented with once you are more confident. There are no right or wrong answers when it comes to debate, so feel free to play with the advice in this book and make it work for you.

The 6-step debate process

The previous chapters introduced you to the six steps that are necessary to prepare a case. We will now apply this process to prepare the proposition case for this difficult and age-old debate topic:

Sample motion: Examinations should be abolished.

Step 1: Understand and define the objective.
Context: Find a recent news article or magazine interview about somebody who failed school examinations yet succeeded in life. Also find a news article about the stresses of exams and how they cause student depression and even suicide. Paint the picture that exams results are thus not a good predictors of life success, and that they harm some students.

Aim: For this debate, we are required to give our opinion as to why exams are so bad that they must be abolished.

Definition: What are examinations, and why do we have them? Examinations are national-level standardised tests that are used to benchmark a student's performance for that year or that phase of education (O-levels, A-levels, SAT). They are often written papers taken under time pressure, usually without the help of textbooks, external notes, or the internet. These exams are graded by staff outside the school, and the grades will determine whether the student advances to the next phase of education or not.

Criteria: The government should abolish exams if it can be proven that they have not achieved their desired outcomes, if there is tangible harm caused to a significant number by retaining them, and if there is a more effective alternative available. Essentially, it should be abolished if it is so terrible that keeping it around does more harm than abolishing it.

Scope: This debate will focus on national-level standardised examinations and not just classroom tests. This debate cannot require the proposition to do away with any form of assessment – exams are a specific form of assessment that have unique failures and we want to abolish just that, not all other forms of in-class assessments.

Step 2: Build a case.

Stakeholders: There are many parties who would be affected by the decision, but only the government actually has the power to make the decision to abolish exams. Governments are motivated by votes (so the desires of parents will matter to them) and by societal benefit, so they would want to choose a system with more good than bad. Furthermore, student suicides – if blamed on government exams – make governments look very bad, so they would want to avoid that situation at all costs.

Case structure: We will structure our case by the criteria for abolition. First argument will be how exams don't work and are unable to be useful indicators of students' capability. Second argument will be about how keeping exams (even as an option) will still result in harm and thus only abolishing exams will work. Third argument will be that there are better alternatives and thus there is no reason why exams cannot and should not be abolished.

Policy or proposal: Replace national examinations with the alternatives proposed.

Case-line: "We must abolish exams because they don't work, they cause harm, and there are better alternatives."

Step 3: Make logical arguments.

For this section, I will focus on one argument: Exams have failed.

Title: Exams have failed to achieve their original purpose. Exams are supposed to measure a student's capability for future success, and provide a benchmark of his or her performance against other students, but exams have not been successful at either task.

Reason: Students' ability is defined as their ability to succeed in the next stage of life – higher education or the working world. Exams test their ability to remember vast quantities of information and provide written responses to questions within a fixed amount of time. Success at university does not require the same set of skills. Success in the working world requires IQ and EQ, and while EQ is wholly untested by exams, even IQ is not properly tested.

Evidence: Many students do exceedingly well in exams but do not do as well in university or later in life (find data to support this). Conversely, a number of high-school dropouts do extremely well in later life, indicating that exams are not useful predictors of capability or success potential.

Significance: Because exams are not useful benchmarks of performance, they have failed in their own original purpose. If they're not even good at what they're supposed to do, why should we still use them?

Step 4: Prepare rebuttal.

Opposition's possible argument: Examinations are an introduction to evaluation, stress, and competition. These issues will arise throughout a person's life, and thus students will benefit from an early exposure to them.

Our rebuttal to this argument: Firstly, studies have shown that examination stress is unique from other life stressors like family or work. Examination stress is unnaturally harsh on the body and mind, especially for a young person, and there is no need for an "early exposure" to such damaging influences. Secondly, even if it wasn't so damaging, there are other ways to "expose" a student to these aspects of life in a more beneficial manner, such as through sports or other extracurricular activities. Thus, examinations do not introduce students to the stresses of real life, are an unnecessarily damaging form of stressors, and there are better and more productive ways of introducing students to competition and stress.

Step 5: Consider interjections.

Interjections depend on the speech of the opposing speaker, and are thus not easy to prepare in advance. However, you can have a short summary of the various counter-studies and other forms of evidence to quickly disprove a claim from the other speaker.

Possible interjection: In 2000, the *Journal of Behavioural Medicine* published findings that the DNA-repair capacity in healthy medical students was reduced during periods of examination stress, more so than during other types of stress. Exams damage our bodies!

Step 6: Consider style.

I would deliver my speech in a more passionate style, to convince audiences that I truly *feel* the pain and stress that some students have to bear, and that the government is needlessly inflicting harm on these poor students. I would balance this passionate style with a rational delivery of how there are better alternatives available, and how the system of exams is "broken" and needs to be fixed. The urgency of the plight of the stressed students must come across clearly and believably to the audience.

The debate speech

In this section, let us draft an opening proposition speaker's speech – for illustration purposes only. You should try to avoid writing speeches once you are comfortable and familiar with the basics of debating.

Using a speaking speed of about 120 words per minute, this speech would last for around six minutes (a little bit of time should be set aside to accept an interjection from the other team). There is no such thing as the perfect debate speech, so please do not assume that this speech is perfect. There will be ways to rebut all the arguments and points below. What this sample speech illustrates is how you should start, build, and end your speech, using the content that we prepared in the previous section.

Introduction

Ladies and Gentlemen, in February 2010, an 11-year-old girl in India named Neha Sawant failed her exams. She hanged herself the next morning. In 1966, a young boy with dyslexia failed his school exams and dropped out of school. His name was Richard Branson, and by 2009 he was the 261st richest person in the world. In one case, a young girl was so overcome by the stress of exams that she killed herself. In the other case, examinations proved to be utterly useless in assessing the capabilities of Richard Branson. How can anybody still defend the system of exams? They *must* be abolished.

Definitions

Examinations are national-level standardised tests that are used to benchmark a student's performance for that year (or that phase of education) against other students. Exams are normally written tests taken under time pressure in large halls, and students must rely on their memory to answer the questions. The grades for these exams will determine whether the student can advance to the next phase of education, or get into a school of their choice. Unlike class tests, exams are normally graded externally and set by a national authority. There are many types of exams, but for today's debate, let's focus on the biggest national-level standardised examinations in Singapore and the U.K. — the O-levels and A-levels.

Defining the objective: Criteria

Governments abolish things when it becomes too harmful to allow them to remain, and if there is a safer and better alternative. Many products fall into this category. We will use this as our criteria for the debate, and prove that examinations should also be abolished.

Team case

Our government must abolish exams because firstly, they are not a useful benchmark of student performance, secondly because retaining exams can cause tangible harm to some students, and thirdly because we believe there are better alternatives. I will cover the first argument, while my second speaker will cover the second and third arguments.

Case-line

We intend to prove that exams must be abolished because they don't work, they cause harm, and there are better alternatives.

First argument: Title

Exams are not useful as a benchmark of performance, and are a terrible predictor of future success.

First argument: Reason

What type of performance do we seek to measure in a student? We want to know whether they will do well in the next stage of life

— whether that is higher education or the working world. Exams measure whether a student can memorise vast quantities of data and write long essays under time pressure. Does that matter at university or in the working world? No. Universities test your ability to comprehend and adapt knowledge, not memorise model answers. The working world requires IQ and EQ to succeed in. Examinations don't test EQ at all, and are not good tests of IQ, because it is possible to score highly in exams even if you don't have a very high IQ (such as through rote learning or model answers).

First argument: Evidence

There have been many studies to show that students who score top marks in exams do not necessarily go on to do well in life. I'll pick an Asian study from China, the world's most populous nation and a fiercely competitive one when it comes to academic achievement. Every year, each batch of graduating high school students goes through the Gaokao (China's national college entrance examination). The media and other students revere the top student of this exam. However, the *China Daily* released an external study in June 2010 that tracked the futures of the 1000 top scorers for the Gaokao since 1977, and the results were clear. Not a single one of them went on to achieve outstanding success in any field. The evidence from other countries is similar: top exam scorers do not always become successful adults.

First argument: Significance

The evidence and logic is thus overwhelmingly clear in this aspect: Examinations are not a useful benchmark and are a terrible predictor of future success. That is the first level of our team case: Exams don't work.

Conclusion

As a team, we will also prove to you later that we must abolish exams and should not retain exams — even as an option — because they can cause harm to students. There are better options available, and we should choose them instead.

For the sake of poor Neha Sawant and the many others who commit suicide from exam stress, for the sake of the students who fail exams and are wrongly told that they have no future because of that, for all their sakes, please agree with the proposition. We must abolish examinations.

Impromptu debates

When preparing a case – whether you have a month, a week, or just an hour to do so – you should always work with a sense of urgency and purpose. As soon as the team receives the motion, the preparation work begins. It is always good to elect a team captain to control the discussions, watch the time, and, most importantly, make the decision when there is an internal disagreement on some issue in the team.

Practise preparing your case within a limited time.

This section illustrates how to prepare a debate case in 60 minutes – but these are only guidelines, not rules.

Individual brainstorming (5 mins)

Each team member should reflect on the motion and come to his own views on the next preparation steps (that is, define the topic and team objective for themselves, team case, etc.). Write down any and all ideas – examples, arguments, case structures, witty introductions

– that come to mind during this phase, so you can share them at the appropriate later stages.

Define the topic and the team's objective (10 mins)

As a team, discuss the motion using the steps in Chapter 2, *Defining the Objective.*

Build the team case. Anticipate the opponent's case (15 mins)

As a team, discuss possible team case structures using the steps in Chapter 3, *Building a Case.* If you are on the opposition side, anticipate what the proposition would do, and see if your case would be able to address that. Work out how the case will be divided between the speakers.

Develop your own arguments individually (20 mins)

Once you have decided as a team what the key arguments are going to be for the case, and who will be taking which arguments, you should break up to individually work on your own arguments using the steps in Chapter 4, *Logical Arguments.*

If you need to prepare rebuttals (because your speaker role requires you to do a lot of rebutting), think through the possible ways to attack the other team's case – and defend your own case – using the steps in Chapter 5, on *Rebuttal.*

Prepare only the skeleton structure – don't write long speeches out in full, because that would be very time consuming and would result in weaker style during the delivery, because you'd just be reading out a speech, instead of speaking to the audience.

Regroup and share – and rehearse (10 mins)

This step is very important but often overlooked. After you have individually prepared your arguments and rebuttals, you should regroup as a team and quickly share what the skeleton outline of your speech looks like. Check that each speaker is consistent with the original team case that was discussed in Step 2 above. If anybody spots any discrepancies or errors in the arguments or evidence, quickly fix it. If you need to rehearse your introduction or a particular argument, ask one of the team members to hear you out and give his feedback. It is particularly important for the first speaker to rehearse in front of the other team members, so that everybody can internalise the team's definitions and case before they step out to the actual debate.

Teamwork on the floor

Teams win debates; don't be individualistic.

One of the greatest dangers of putting a group of confident, intelligent individuals into the same debate team is that they can let their individual egos overpower the team. Always remember: you are part of a team. Like in any team sport, you must learn to play your part, even if it sometimes means letting somebody else get the credit in order for your team to win.

Share with one another during the debate.

Pass notes, whisper, or do whatever is allowed in order to help your teammate shine when they get the microphone. Don't be selfish about keeping a clever example for yourself so that you can use it later on in your own speech — it might be too late by then to convince the judges.

Don't undermine your teammates while they are on stage.

If your teammate makes a mistake, or says something that you didn't expect him to say, don't look shocked, angry or exasperated. Judges can see your reaction, even though you might be sitting in

9

COACHING AND TEACHING

"A good coach will make his players see what they can be rather than what they are."

— ARA PARSEGHIAN, one of the most successful coaches of Notre Dame University's collegiate football team

---

As a coach and teacher, you are often responsible for the development and success of a student debate team – and that can be a daunting responsibility. One of the most critical lessons I teach all coaches is this: Before you give them homework, make sure you've done your *own* homework. Know the rules, research the topics, and watch lots of debates. Be a professional, and love the sport. Teach your team to believe in themselves and love the sport, and you can't go wrong as a coach.

Selecting a debate team

Debaters do not all come from the same mould. Some debaters are fiercely competitive; others are laid-back. Some are outspoken and argumentative; others are calm and chilled-out. Some are confident speakers; others are introverts by nature. Do not assume that all debaters must fit a certain stereotype when selecting your school debate team.

Different debate formats have different rules. As a team coach, it is your responsibility to understand the roles, scoring criteria, etc. For the purposes of this chapter, I will rely on the WSDC format and rules; the principles, however, are generic and thus easily transferable to any other debating format.

Use intra-school debates to pick speakers.

If you would like to sift out the best potential student debaters, having an inter-class competition, judged by teachers, will be sufficient for you to evaluate who the potential "natural" debaters are. This approach is meritocratic and will expose good talent, but may not encourage some of the less proficient (but nonetheless eager-to-learn) students to participate in debates.

Hold an open audition.

Alternatively, if you would like to adopt a more egalitarian selection process, you can hold an open audition or try-out. The try-out can be broken down into two stages: a written portion, where the student is assessed for basic comprehension and critical analysis of simple written arguments; and an oral interview, in which a teacher converses with the student on a topic to assess his speaking ability and ability to "think on their feet." This method is more open, especially for quieter students who may be "diamonds in the rough," but unless your school has a strong emphasis on debating, you may not find a lot of willing participants.

Select a variety of speakers.

A team consists of three speakers (for the WSDC format of debates). Typically, the first speaker is a good orator, while the third speaker is a clever argumentative debater. Selecting a well-balanced team – some good orators and some clever arguers – is important, especially if you cannot find a lot of students who are masters of both.

Select enough students for a sparring team as well.

Select at least two teams' worth of students so that you have ready sparring partners for your "first team" of debaters. This way you also have enough reserves for each position in case any of the students in your "first team" is unable to compete at the last minute.

Training for content

Compile background briefs for emerging issues and likely topics.

This is necessary to ensure that the debaters are kept up to date on the key topics in the news and on the different subject areas that may be debated. Websites like Wikipedia provide a great introduction to most issues. Every debate team should have at least a basic understanding of key concepts in science, technology, anthropology, criminology and law, economics, philosophy, politics, psychology, sociology and other important areas of human knowledge.

Brainy game show

Write down about seven questions and answers in five categories. The categories should cut across different knowledge areas, such as politics, technology, current affairs, and so on. Read out the question, and the first student who "buzzes in" (or raises his hand) gets to answer. Correct answers will gain the student points, wrong answers lose him points. This activity tests students' general knowledge.

Lightning preparation

Prepare a list of motions across a variety of areas, and provide each student with the list. Ask the students to very briefly write down the following for the proposition (or opposition): (1) the aim of the debate, (2) the criteria for the case, (3) a simple 3-argument case structure. Give them 15 minutes to complete the above for as many motions as they can. This activity trains students to quickly grasp the key requirements and issues for a debate motion or topic.

Lightning arguments

Give the student a debate topic and a side. The student should think of a single full argument complete with a title, a reason, some evidence, and significance within one minute. After one minute, the speaker must deliver a full argument. Due to the short preparation time available, you can allow students to "fabricate" the evidence as long as it is believable – the goal of this exercise is not to test their knowledge of evidence, but to train them to develop arguments quickly.

Alley/Zig-Zag debates

Break the students into two groups, and have them stagger themselves in a zig-zag formation. Announce a debate topic, and deliver a prepared argument for the topic. The first student in the zig-zag formation must rebut your argument. The second speaker in the zig-zag must defend your argument and/or rebut the first speaker. The third speaker must rebut the second and/or defend the first, and so on. Keep the zig-zag to fewer than six people for maximum impact. This activity trains students to constantly find the flaws in every argument.

Rebut blogs, magazine articles, newspapers, forum letters

Prepare a bag of short articles on a topic from a variety of sources. Ask each student to pick one of the articles, and give them a few minutes to read and analyse the article. Students must find the flaws in the article, and then deliver a persuasive counter-case and rebuttal of the article.

Training for style

Watch and learn from famous speakers.

Make the students watch a video of a famous speaker without the sound. Ask them to identify the positive and persuasive elements of the speaker's style. Ask them to watch videos of bad speakers (such as those from a novice debate competition), and identify the negative style elements.

Eliminate verbal crutches and fillers.

Use video recordings to point out and reduce the use of verbal crutches like "uh," "hmm," "like," "Ladies and Gentlemen," etc. Tell them to replace those verbal fillers with a pause, if they need time to think. Students can practise by delivering impromptu speeches until they are able to eliminate verbal crutches. As a training activity, you can ask other students to count the number of verbal crutches that a speaker used per minute of speaking.

Experiment with different introductions and conclusions.

Ask students to experiment with the different types of introductions and conclusions (discussed in the earlier chapter on style) for the same debate motion. The other students can vote on which introduction and conclusion was the most persuasive and attention-grabbing.

Game: Just-a-minute (JAM)

This activity gives students the confidence to speak on any topic without preparation, and trains them to avoid using verbal crutches. Pick a student to speak. Ask the other students to provide a random topic ("Elephants in Africa"). The student must then deliver a one-minute speech on the topic. If the student uses "uh," "mmm" or any other time-wasting verbal crutches pre-identified by the coach, any of the other students can yell "Jam!" and interrupt the speaker. The speaker is then replaced by the other student who yelled "Jam," and the clock continues from where the previous speaker left off. The same rules continue to apply – if this new speaker goes off topic, or uses any time-wasting words, the other students (including the original speaker) can yell "Jam" and him. The goal of the game is to be the person speaking when the one-minute buzzer goes off.

Record their voices.

This activity teaches students to be aware of their vocal problems. Record their voices and play it back to them. Ask them to list the ways their voices could be improved. If they are speaking too fast, ask them to practise delivering a speech of 120 words in exactly one minute, to slow them down. If their voice is too high-pitched, ask them to pretend they are singing and deliver the speech in a deep baritone singing voice. Over time, they can incorporate these into their natural vocal range.

Game: To be or not to be?

This activity trains students' vocal technique and ability to "create" a debate persona. Ask students to reproduce dialogue from famous books or plays "in character." (Shakespeare is always a great choice.) The student must imagine what the character would sound like, and create a persona and voice for the character. The other students should judge the performance.

Game: Guess the speaker

This activity broadens students' style repertoire. Prepare short videos of five different famous speakers. Ask a student to randomly select one and watch it without letting the other students see which speaker was selected. Then ask the student to reproduce a generic debate speech (not the speech that the famous speaker delivered) using the style of the famous speaker. The other students must guess which of the five famous speakers the performer is mimicking.

Game: Mood scales 1–10

This activity builds emotional and vocal range in speech delivery. Give the students a pre-written speech, and ask them to read out the speech in a certain mood (angry, happy, sad, etc.). Give the most extreme state (that is, the "angriest") a value of 10, and the most passive state (that is, the "least angry) a value of 1. The student should start reading the speech from an emotional state "value" of 1, and move up to 10 on your command. Once they have gone from 1 to 10, randomly interject their speech with a new value, and they should seamlessly transition their emotional state to the new value. For more advanced students, you can ask them to transition between different emotional states (for example, go from an "Angry 7" to a "Happy 3" to a "Sad 10"). The other students should judge the performance, or (for the advanced students) guess what states the student is transitioning between.

Game: Negative-style Bingo

This activity trains students to minimise "negative" posture and distracting gestures. Make a video recording of them delivering a speech naturally, and go through the video with them. Write down the list of flaws on a whiteboard for the class to note. Ask the student to repeat the speech in front of the class again, but this time, whenever the debater makes one of the mistakes on the list, the other students should shout "Bingo!" and the debater has to stop. The student who is able to speak for the longest time wins this game.

Build team strategy by explaining how each debater's role fits together in the team for the competition.

Every speaker on the team must know his role in the team, and be able to fulfil it in a way that is most persuasive. Each student must be very familiar with his basic responsibilities in the team. Study the table on the following page (based on the WSDC format) — getting these basics correct will give your team a good strategy score.

Team training

The best training for a team is a spar debate.

Individual exercises to train style and content are useful, but debate strategy is best taught using an actual debate. Furthermore, exposing students more regularly to the stress of time pressure and public speaking makes them more comfortable with extraneous elements – such as phones ringing, lights flickering, people moving about in the background – so over time they stop worrying about "public speaking" and are able to focus more clearly on the debate topic and the other side's arguments.

Make your debate team spar against your reserve team (or against other schools) as much as possible. Enter them into smaller debate competitions; make them do exhibition debates in front of

	Proposition	Opposition
First speaker	• Define the motion • Explain the Prop team case • Explain how each speaker will add to the team's case • Start the Prop case with one or two arguments	• Rebut the definition or Prop case (only if required) • Rebut major points in 1st Prop case • Explain the Opp team case • Explain how each speaker will add to the team's case • Start the Opp case with one or two arguments
Second speaker	• Rebut 1st Opp case • Defend 1st Prop case • Further the Prop case with one or two arguments	• Rebut Prop case • Defend Opp case • Further the Opp case with one or two arguments
Third speaker	• Rebut 1st and 2nd Opp case • Defend 1st and 2nd Prop case	• Rebut Prop case • Defend Opp case
Reply speaker	• Summarise the key reasons why the Prop should win the debate	• Summarise the key reasons why the Opp should win the debate

the school. All of these activities will build resilience to the stresses of debating, which comes in very handy during major competitions.

Research both sides of the spar debate topic.

As a coach, you will be better placed to evaluate the quality and diversity of arguments raised by the teams if you have done your own homework and researched the topic, the arguments, and the evidence beforehand. Watch how other teams have debated similar topics (there are plenty of school debate videos online), and see how they choose to attack the topic.

Decide on speaker positions for each debater.

Some coaches like to put their strongest speaker at the start, so the case is clear and persuasive from the outset. Others prefer to put their weakest debater up-front, because there are fewer rebuttals to deal with, and the large part of the case can be prepared in advance. Likewise, which debater to put in second or third positions (and for WSDC, which speaker should give the reply speech) is a critical decision that a coach must make. There is no right or wrong answer. As a coach, you should feel free to experiment by rotating your debaters into different positions for the spar debates. On the one hand, it is useful to develop "specialised" speakers – that is, consistently train a debater to master a particular role (for example, the case set-up and definition roles for a first speaker). On the other hand, cross-training a debater between the various positions builds a more well-rounded debater, and they will then have a more holistic appreciation of how a team can work more closely together because they understand the challenges of each part.

Keep a log of each speaker's problems.

Every spar debate builds on the previous training session. Keep a running log record of the various mistakes and errors that have been made by the speakers in the previous debates, and let them know in advance what those are. Advise them first on what they should avoid doing (or be doing more of) before the debate starts. The log also allows you to monitor your debaters' progress over time.

Give them the topic and team sides, set a fixed preparation time, and then let them debate.

Once you assign the motion and sides, let the teams prepare their cases – without your participation. You should, however, hover and observe their preparation from a distance and record any issues or problems that you find, but save the comments until after the debate ends and you are providing your full debrief to the students. Examples of problems that might happen during preparation: one student dominates the discussion and drowns out other ideas; the team is unable to reach a quick consensus on the basic case-line; they spend too much time brainstorming new arguments and too little time developing the supporting structure (reasons and evidence) for their arguments. Many coaches also choose to video-record the preparation session in addition to the debate itself, so that students can review their own mistakes for themselves.

Debrief the teams thoroughly after the debate.

The debrief should cover all aspects of the team's performance, starting from the important big issues, and then zooming in on each of the more specific and individual issues.

Which issues mattered most and least in the debate?

Start your debrief by analysing whether the teams understood which were the *most important* issues, and which issues were more peripheral to the outcome of the debate. If a team could only run one single argument to win the case, which argument would that be? Once you have helped the team identify the key points, analyse whether they were sufficiently well-explained and substantiated, or whether it could have been done better – and how. If they had to rank their arguments in order of importance, which would be the lowest ranking argument? Was that argument necessary, or was it a divergent thread that could have been removed from their speeches? Were there issues that were not raised at all that could have been useful in arguing for or against the motion?

Training and focusing a team using this post-mortem is an effective way of teaching a team to analyse a motion, prioritise their arguments, and distinguish critical points from the red herrings.

How did each debater live up to his role and potential?

This part of the debrief will require you to go into the specific and individual issues. How did each speaker fare in terms of content, style, and strategy? How could they improve in each of those areas, and what specific mistakes did they make? Training is the best time for you to provide constructive criticism for the students to learn.

Be specific in your advice; vague demands are unhelpful.

One of the critical failings of most coaches is their inability to articulate clearly and specifically what was wrong and how it could be improved. Vague demands such as "Come up with better rebuttals!" or, worse, "Be more persuasive!" are utterly unhelpful. List specific mistakes and provide examples to illustrate what you expect of them instead. Let them know what they said, why it was wrong, and provide them a better version, taking care to explain to them why this version is better.

Debate in the classroom

Debate is not just for school teams.

Integrating debate-related activities into the classroom teaches non-debaters the useful life skills that debaters possess. However, this is no small challenge, for a number of reasons. Non-debaters are often quite shy, and may not be willing to share their views easily. They may also be less well-informed about issues, and thus not have any strong opinions of their own yet. Classrooms are also much larger compared to the ten students you would be coaching in two debate teams. And because of the tight schedules that classes are run on, there is much less time during a class lesson than during a debate coaching session. For all these reasons, debates must be adapted and modified to suit the classroom setting.

Make them have opinions: Play "Pick a side."

Debate is a daunting and frightening activity for many young students – even if they possess the raw natural talent for speaking. Many of them are not used to having a strong opinion or point of view on a particular issue. This introductory activity, "Pick a side," gives students a first taste of the basics of debate: having to defend an opinion.

Get the students to stand around in a group. Draw an imaginary line to divide the room in half. Announce a simple topic, such as "School uniforms should be abolished," or "Children should not be allowed on the internet without adult supervision." Explain that those in agreement with the topic should move to one side of the room and those who oppose the topic should move to the other side (for clarity's sake, announce in advance which half of the room represents the proposition and opposition). Students must immediately go to one side or the other. Once all students have moved, ask each student to list one reason for his choosing that side. Disallow students from repeating reasons – this will encourage them to speak earlier rather than later, and will also force them to think on their feet rather than just agree with the previous students' reasons. This activity builds up their self-confidence and ability to rationalise their opinions and viewpoints.

Make them defend their opinions: Teach the basic structure of an argument to all students.

Students who have never been taught to debate may not be aware of the basic structure of an argument, and may thus have an irrational fear that arguments must be very complex or may be beyond their abilities. Explain to them that an argument can be very simple – consisting of a *title*, a *reason*, some *evidence*, and a conclusion that states the *significance* of the argument. A simple four-sentence argument (that is, one sentence for each aspect) is sufficient and simple enough for non-debaters to grasp.

Make them research their opinions: Assign homework essays.

There is not enough time in a single class for the students to research and develop their arguments fully. To maximise classroom time, they should spend the class session coming up with a simple four-sentence argument, then take that home to further research and develop. The students can write short essays to defend their opinion.

Make them present their opinions orally.

Teach the students the basics components of style, and ask them to read out their essays in class. While debaters rarely read out pre-written speeches, most students are not yet confident enough to deliver an off-the-cuff speech (even if they have already done the research). Allow the students to read out their short essays in front of the class, and encourage them to ad-lib and improvise as much as possible. Give the students private debriefs (written or face-to-face) rather than commenting on their speeches directly after they speak, as non-debaters may be less open to accepting criticism on their speaking style in front of other students.

Coaching philosophy

Being a coach of a debate team is a huge responsibility. Coaches are entrusted with more than just the competition performance of a debate team – they are often required to look after the intellectual and emotional development of their students, because good debaters must be taught how to think analytically and speak with confidence (which requires them to have self-confidence and often some level of emotional strength). Coaching a debate team thus often comes with a lot of hidden challenges – teenagers are often lacking in self-confidence, and need to be carefully nurtured and groomed to reach their full potential.

Don't be mean.

Some sports coaches think that "tough love" is the best way to teach their team – yelling at them, scolding them, and even shaming them into performing better as a team. I had a hockey coach like that once, and it was not pleasant. Debate coaches should never adopt that approach. Debating requires confidence (which translates to good style), so shattering their self-confidence during training sessions is counter-productive. Offer constructive criticism, and explain to them that your goal is to help them learn from their mistakes in an open environment, not to insult or shame them.

Cultivate intellectual curiosity and passion.

I've found that like in most activities, those who do best in debating are the ones who are truly passionate about it. Help your team develop a passion for debate, and encourage their efforts to read more widely, discuss controversial topics regularly, watch a diversity of speakers, and participate in any debate-related activities such as public speaking or drama. Students who enjoy being on stage and enjoy being intellectually curious will naturally love debating more.

Don't burn the kids out by over-stressing them.

Some stress and some competitive pressure is always good – they keep the students on their toes and make them want to improve after each debate. However, too much stress and emphasis on winning may backfire. Teams that lose may become emotionally distraught and thus unable to take the loss as a "learning lesson" for future improvements. I've seen teams break down and cry for hours because they lost a debate, and their coaches, rather than encouraging them that it's not the end of the world, make it worse by chastising them for doing so poorly. Teams that get so emotional after a loss will burn out quickly. Even good teams sometimes lose debates, but they should learn to be good sportsmen.

Don't shy away from moral dilemmas just because they are young or because you have a personal opinion on the topic.

Some socially conservative teachers and coaches avoid discussing controversial issues like prostitution, pre-marital sex and abortion, because these go against their own moral beliefs. Debaters should not be "forced" to accept any version of truth or morality; they should be allowed to ask difficult questions about the morality or immorality of social actions, and be able to discuss both sides of the issue rationally, whatever their personal beliefs. Just because the teacher's/coach's/debater's religious beliefs or family upbringing has taught them that a particular act is immoral does not mean that they should take an irrationally harsh view on the topic. Debaters should always believe in free speech, because it is only by analysing both sides of an issue that we can come to a deeper understanding ourselves. Besides, they may have to fight for the opposite side (to their own belief) some day, so they have no choice!

> *"I disapprove of what you say, but I will defend to the death your right to say it."*
>
> – Attributed to VOLTAIRE

JUDGING

"I look to a day when people will not be judged by the colour of their skin, but by the content of their character."

— MARTIN LUTHER KING, JR.

"They misunderestimated me."

— GEORGE W. BUSH

WE PLAY THE ROLE of judge as often as we do the role of a debater. We are constantly evaluating the information we receive from other people. Our "inner judge" is constantly assessing the world around us, and helping us to decide what is right and wrong and come to a verdict on important issues.

Learning to judge a debate is an important skill, because you see the speeches through a critical lens. You learn to be fair and impartial, and judge the issue based on the merit of the arguments, not on your preconceived biases. In Martin Luther King, Jr.'s case, that would be his dream come true. In George W. Bush's case, he's happy if you don't "misunderestimate" him – whatever that means.

The role of the judge

A judge decides who wins and who loses the debate.

Debating is a competitive activity, with winners and losers. Most formats don't allow draws or ties – one team must win and another must lose. A debate judge, or adjudicator, is the person entrusted to make that decision on who wins and who loses. Judges are often experienced debaters themselves, and are thus familiar with the rules and expectations of the debate. Most tournaments run an adjudicator-training workshop prior to the start of the debates, to ensure that all judges are up to the mark. If you are interested in becoming a judge, contact the tournament organiser and ask them about adjudication training.

A judge's personal opinion on the topic is irrelevant.

It does not matter whether you as the judge personally agree or disagree with the topic. If you are personally against the death penalty and happen to be judging a debate on the same topic, your personal bias should not, in any way, affect your decision on who won or who lost the debate. This is very difficult to ensure, and judges who know they have a strong personal opinion on the topic must consciously try and let go of their "baggage" and listen to the arguments of both teams objectively. If you feel like your personal opinions on the topic are overwhelming to the point that you cannot be unbiased, excuse yourself from the role of adjudicator for that debate and ask the tournament organisers to find a replacement.

The winner may be determined by a single judge, a panel of independent judges, or by concurrence from multiple judges.

The organisers will determine in advance whether a lone judge or a panel of judges will judge the debates. If you are judging a debate alone, your verdict will be the sole determinant of the outcome.

If there are other judges with you, then there are two ways in which the final outcome may be arrived at. In formats like the WSDC, the judges are treated as individual and independent, and each of their verdicts (or "ballots") counts as a "vote" for that team. In a panel of three adjudicators, if two judges vote for the proposition team and the third judge decides in favour of the opposition team, then the proposition team wins because it had more votes. This obviously requires an odd number of judges so that there is never a tie.

Other formats – such as the British Parliamentary format – consider the judges as a single entity that must come up with a consolidated decision after discussion. That is, they are allowed to confer after the debate, and must agree on the winner *as a panel*.

A judge awards scores to the speakers and teams.

Depending on the format and rules of the competition, a judge must award a certain grade or score to each speaker and to the team as a whole. Obviously, the winning team must get the highest score or grade. Each format of debate has its own criteria for scoring, and often some amount of training and understudying is required in order to be able to assess how high or low to score a speaker.

A judge delivers the verdict to the teams.

Just like in the legal context, a debate judge is also responsible for explaining the reasons for his or her verdict. The judge cannot simply say, "The Proposition won," and leave it at that. Debaters are argumentative people, and the opposition team is certainly going to challenge you to explain why they lost.

Sometimes different judges see a debate differently.

Persuasion is a very subjective issue, and even though score-sheets attempt to break down persuasion into different subcategories (style, content, strategy, etc.), it is still highly personal. Each judge may have a slightly different perspective on what happened during the debate, what mattered most, and what was most persuasive. Even if all the judges are perfectly unbiased, their individual interpretations of the debates may differ because no two humans think exactly alike. Don't be worried if the adjudicators in the room give different verdicts or different scores — as long as they all have followed the rules and have given scores that are aligned with the instructions provided during the adjudicator training, it's okay. If you are a dissenting adjudicator (that is, you were one of the judges in the minority who voted for the losing team), don't worry. Judges do not need to be unanimous — that's why we have panels of multiple adjudicators.

Philosophies of judging

Different formats have different judging philosophies.

In a debate competition, the two sides and the debate speakers are not the only participants in the debate. In most formats of debate, the judge plays a very large role as well – and thus there is a need to discuss the "philosophies" that govern how an adjudicator should play his role in the debate. In this section, we discuss three of the more common philosophies.

Philosophy 1: The judge is a "blank slate" who does not do any analysis on his own.

In this philosophy, the judge believes everything that he hears from the debaters, and will not question the truth or logic of the argument unless the other team raises it. This judge is a "blank slate," who is just waiting to absorb the speeches from the debaters. He comes with no prior knowledge of the topic and no ability to counter-check the facts or arguments, and relies purely on the other teams to disprove the points. If the other team fails to rebut any particular point, this type of judge will continue to believe that the particular point is true – even if any ordinary intelligent person would know that the point is false or illogical. Very few debate competitions encourage this style of adjudication, so if you encounter a judge like this, it may be possible that the judge is actually, in fact, vacuous.

Philosophy 2: The judge is the "next opponent speaker," waiting to rebut every point with his expert knowledge.

Competitions that encourage a high level of research into a particular topic area (such as International Humanitarian Law debates), or that are based on a particular framework of argumentation (for example, moot or legal debates that use domestic laws as the framework) often ask judges to play the role of "subject specialist." The judge is thus very well-read on the topic and able to distinguish between facts and fibs even before the opponent speaker points it out. The judge plays an interventionist role in the scoring, by analysing your argument for flaws and scoring you accordingly. The judge can be thought of as the "hidden opponent speaker," who does not need to wait for the other team to point out your shortcomings and loopholes. Again, most debate competitions avoid this style of adjudication, because it means that the judge has "stepped in" to the debate and become a participant in the debate and is thus no longer a neutral assessor.

Philosophy 3: The judge is a rational, intelligent, reasonable, unbiased and generally well-read person.

This is the middle-ground between the two philosophies above, and also the most commonly used adjudication style in competitions. It requires a judges to just be himself: intelligent and rational enough to be able to distinguish good logic from bad arguments; well-read enough to know the key facts and issues but not a subject-matter-expert on the topic; and, most importantly, a reasonable and unbiased "man on the street." The judge should not "step in" to the debate and pretend to be the opponent, but they should also not blindly accept everything that is being said by the speakers if they know that it is false. It is obviously a delicate balance – how "well-read" should the judge be before it borders on subject expertise? How rational and intelligent should they be in analysing the points before they become the "opponent in waiting"? These are tricky balances that must be learned through experience. Most debate competitions ask adjudicators to adopt this model of thinking.

Preparation before the debate

Judges must understand the rules of the debate format.

Studying and understanding the rules of the competition you are about to judge is critical. You should know what to expect from the debate (in terms of the speaking order, duration of speeches, number of teams, etc.) and also what is allowed and disallowed in the debate you are about to judge. In some formats of debate, the other teams are actually allowed to heckle the speaker – and you are expected as a judge to just ignore it. If you didn't know that heckling was allowed, you might get quite startled when one of the debaters started shouting "Boo! Shame!" midway through another speaker's speech!

Judges must be familiar with the scoring criteria.

Since you are required to grade the teams and the speakers, you should have some familiarity with the scoring standards and what a "good" speaker would look and sound like. You should preferably have watched a debate in this format, for example on video, and been briefed on how to score that speaker, so that you can make a good assessment of how the speakers you are about to judge would score, in relation to that video.

Judges should be at least as familiar with the topic as the average "man on the street."

You shouldn't try to become a subject-matter expert in every debate topic. However, if there are areas of common knowledge that you have always been weak in, now is the time for you to brush up on them. If you are a passionate literature student and the term "genetic engineering" means nothing to you because you slept through all your biology classes, you might want to go and browse the web for some intro articles. If you have trouble finding the Middle East on a map, you might want to educate yourself on the region a bit more, just in case you are required to judge a debate topic on the political or religious conflicts within that region.

> "*Success depends upon previous preparation, and without such preparation there is sure to be failure.*"
>
> — CONFUCIUS

Judging a debate

Listen and watch the debater closely and write down the important aspects of the speech.

To judge a speaker on content and style, you must have a system to write down your observations and analysis of his content and style. This will help you to score his speech at the end of the speech, and, if necessary, amend his scores at the end of the debate. Most judges develop their own system for "tracking" the debate – that is, writing down the speaker's speech and adding comments. I use multiple pen colours to differentiate between the speaker's key points, my quick analysis of the points, and my comments on his style.

Analyse the arguments – weak ones deserve little credit.

Arguments are weak if they do not meet the expectations of a "good" argument, as set out in earlier chapters, and are thus unconvincing. You should penalise debaters for making weak arguments.

If the other team rebuts the weak argument, reward the other team. If the other team does not rebut it, that does not mean that the weak point deserves higher credit; it is still a weak point. It just means that the other team dropped an opportunity to rebut a weak argument. Whether or not you penalise the other team for dropping this rebuttal depends on the adjudication philosophy of the competition, but generally speaking, it shows that the other team was not able to maximise the "attack" on their opponents. Any team that does not robustly attack the weaknesses in the other team's case normally should be penalised.

Constantly question if you are bringing in personal biases.

As a judge, you must always be vigilant that you are judging the debate based on the debate itself, and not bringing in your personal biases. Don't imagine how you could have or would have attacked or presented an argument. Don't compare the student debaters against your own (probably excellent) skills as a debater. Judge the debate; don't "join" the debate.

Score the overall impact of the speaker, rather than adding or subtracting marks for each good or bad thing they do.

If a speech contains great arguments but no rebuttals, you should reward the speaker for the great examples and penalise him for the lack of rebuttals. The final score should be determined by how effective the speech was *as a whole* and not on piecemeal evaluation of each item. If the speaker started with a very engaging style but towards the end became nervous and lost the audience, consider if his overall speech was less engaging because the end was so bad? Or was his introduction so compelling that the bad ending was inconsequential? Judge the debater on the overall impact and effect of his speech.

There is no such thing as an "automatic loss."

Just like scoring a speaker, you should judge a team based on the overall effect of the team. Teams cannot win or lose for just one thing. You should evaluate the teams as a whole and judge all the relevant factors for the debate when making your decision.

Cross-check your scores across speakers and categories.

Your scores should reflect the relativity of the performance between each aspect of the debate. Comparing the team scores, the team with the higher score should be the team that won the debate (if not, there is something wrong with the way you scored the teams or judged the debate). Comparing the different speakers, the speakers who got the higher scores should be the speakers who were more persuasive and gave better speeches. Comparing the different elements *within* a speaker's speech (such as style, content, strategy), the breakdown should reflect that speaker's strengths and weaknesses. Furthermore, the breakdown of the different elements *across* different speakers should make sense as well – if you felt one speaker had a better style than another speaker, then that speaker's style score should be higher than the other speaker's.

Do not underestimate the difficulty of judging a debate.
Students put in a lot of effort to prepare themselves for a competitive debate, and thus you should expect the outcome to be very important (and sometimes emotional) for them. When the opposing teams are closely matched, your talent as a judge will make all the difference. You need to put in effort to listen, analyse, and evaluate the debates so that you reach the correct decision. This is hard work, and you should only be an adjudicator if you are willing and able to put in the effort to do it right.

Delivering the verdict

Delivering the verdict serves three very important purposes.
The key purposes of the verdict are (1) to announce who won the debate; (2) to explain the rationale behind this decision; and (3) to highlight – and commend, if required – speakers for good and bad aspects in the debate. Judges sometimes offer suggestions on how the debate could have been improved, but this is an optional item.

As an adjudicator, you will usually have three opportunities to provide feedback and comments for a debate: (1) written feedback on your score-sheet, which is often sent to the teams after the competition; (2) oral feedback when you deliver the verdict; and (3) individual briefings to the teams and speakers after the debate – sometimes teams or speakers approach the judges after the debate and request for explanations or advice.

The chief adjudicator normally explains the decision.
If you are the chief adjudicator, how should you deliver a good oral adjudication summary? This section provides some pointers, but keep in mind that all debates are different and a model answer on oral summaries cannot be given.

Jot down key points as they occur to you during the debate.
Prepare your notes early. You can start jotting down key factors that should be raised in the oral summary even during the debate. This would mean that you are unlikely to forget key points that were raised earlier in the debate. In the same vein, this would make the deliberations with the panel quicker. When preparing your notes, you can also start to categorise your points so that they are already be in your preferred order when you deliver the summary.

If you are representing a panel of judges, include their views.
You can seek their opinions during the post-debate discussion before the verdict is announced. On some contentious areas, it would important to highlight both the majority *and* the dissenting views. If you already have the preferred order of points for adjudication, it is easy to slot the additional points into your delivery.

Keep the audience in mind when delivering your verdict.
The oral adjudication summary is your only opportunity to address the audience, whereas there is still another chance to engage the debaters later, when you debrief the teams individually. Stick to the key issues without getting into the intricate details that would be best brought up later when talking with the teams.

Keep it short and precise.
Stick to the key issues; don't ramble on. There should be the same time discipline that is expected of the speakers. Before delivering the

speech, estimate how long it would take to deliver the summary and try to stick to that time limit.

Depending on the format of the debate and the competition, the verdict may be given either before or after the oral adjudication summary. There is a tendency to keep the comments vague so that the verdict will come as a surprise. Try to avoid this – vague comments do not provide learning points for the audience and the teams. If a good oral adjudication is delivered, the audience would be able to see what the key considerations for the decision were and the verdict will not be a surprise.

Keep your comments positive; don't focus on the negative.

Debaters are young students – don't mock them or criticise them in front of the audience. The goal of your post-debate remarks is to help them improve and learn from their mistakes, not to rub salt in the losing team's wounds, or to demoralise the winning team by criticising their efforts. You may have been a great debater in your days, but this is not the chance for you to show off how clever you are; focus your brilliance on helping the young debaters learn and grow for their next debate.

Common mistakes

This section lists the common mistakes that some inexperienced adjudicators make, and that you should try to avoid.

Mistake: Failing to recognise your own deep-rooted biases.

When a topic is controversial and goes against your religious or societal perspective, you must be very cautious. Some judges are unable to recognise that they have a natural inclination towards one side, and end up over-crediting the team that sides with their beliefs.

This is wrong. You must be impartial and objective, even if it means going against your beliefs. If you feel so strongly about a topic that you think you may not be able to overcome your beliefs, excuse yourself from that debate.

Some judges make the opposite mistake. Knowing they have a personal bias, they over-compensate for this and over-credit the opposing team, to "prove" that they were unbiased.

Mistake: Having favourites.

As a judge, you must put aside any relationship or friendship that you have with any of the debaters, and any feelings you have towards any of the teams. After a few years of judging, you may find you have judged the same school team or the same debaters many times. You must not let your past interactions with the teams or debaters influence your assessment of the current debate. Just because they were amazing debaters last year does not mean that they will be amazing in this debate, and so you should not think that "they will definitely win" this debate. If you do not think you are able to put aside your personal preferences, or if your relationship with the teams is too close, you should excuse yourself as an adjudicator and get a replacement judge.

Mistake: Bringing in expert knowledge that most people would not know or understand.

No matter which adjudication philosophy is chosen, there is some knowledge that is so obscure that most people would never know or understand it. If you are asked to judge a debate, and you happen to be the leading academic authority on the topic, do not expect student debaters to have the same level of depth and understanding as you do on that topic. Judge them based on what you would expect from a reasonably intelligent person who has read the different theories on the topic. If you know the obscure and complex counter-arguments to conventional wisdom, you should not penalise teams for not raising them – you may want to educate teams *after* the debate, but it should not impact your scoring.

Mistake: Speaking in "debaterese" only.

Be clear and specific in your feedback. Using debate jargon (or "debaterese") is not useful because it masks the problem in technical terminology. If you think they could have defined the topic better, tell them directly what the problem with the definition was and why you think it could have been better. Using technical terms that are familiar among advanced debaters – for example, "tiered sub-contentions," "signposting," or "claris" – may confuse novice debaters.

Mistake: Placing unfair expectations on the debaters.

If you were an excellent debater (as most judges tend to be), it is likely that you will have your own way of winning a debate on any given topic. Do not expect teams to think exactly like you – they may have their own way of developing a case, and you should allow them to do so.

Mistake: Penalising speakers for their accents.

This is a big no-no, especially for international debate competitions involving many different countries. Even for domestic competitions, there is an increasing ethnic diversity in each country. Just because a debater from China or Australia pronounces a word differently from how you would – or because they have a slightly different way of constructing sentences – does not make it wrong. As long as they are able to get their message across and capture the attention of the audience, you should not penalise speakers for their accents.

Mistake: Being mean.

Don't verbally abuse the debaters. Be constructive in your criticism, and balance it with compliments on things that the speakers did well and should continue doing. Students have fragile egos, and you should be building up their self-confidence, not destroying it.

Mistake: Being unprofessional and disrespectful.

If you are affiliated in any way with one of the teams you are judging (perhaps you have a sibling in the team, or you are an alumni), you should highlight this to both teams and to the chief adjudicator. The right thing to do when conflicts of interest arise is to find another adjudicator. It is your responsibility to be professional and make sure that the students perceive you to be an unbiased and fair judge at all times.

Don't be disrespectful to the debaters. Avoid texting on your phone, sleeping, doodling, and any other activity that is not related to your job as a judge.

Mistake: Disrespecting the other judges.

If you are a dissenting judge, do not mock or scoff at the opinions of the other judges. If you are in the majority, do not put down or insult the dissenting judges. Each judge is entitled to his or her own opinion, and your rants against the other judges will reflect worse on your own character than their ability as judges. If you have a legitimate complaint against one of the other judges, go to the chief adjudicator or organiser. Don't whine to the debaters.

Mistake: Getting into an argument with the students.

As a judge, you should maintain a cool, calm, and mature composure when debriefing the students. Even if they get upset (as losing teams sometimes do) you should keep your cool. Explain your position, but don't feel cornered or pressured if they keep badgering you for answers. Debaters are argumentative, but don't fall into the trap of arguing with them. If they have a complaint about your performance as a judge, they should take it to the organisers.

Mistake: Thinking that you never make mistakes.
You may be an experienced judge, but it does not make your judgment perfect all the time. Be prepared to defend your opinion and assessment of the debate (vigorously, if you must) but if the chief adjudicator or other judges have some feedback from you, listen to them. Handle complaints graciously when you do receive them. Learn from your mistakes.

Being an adjudicator is a great opportunity to infuse young debaters with passion for the activity. Relish the role and respect the responsibilities!

11

APPLYING DEBATE-THINKING EVERY DAY

"Don't back down just to keep the peace. Standing up for your beliefs builds self-confidence and self-esteem."

— OPRAH WINFREY, a former school debater

THE EARLIER CHAPTERS in this book have taught you the skills that I call "Debate-thinking." These methodologies and thought processes can form the basis for the content of almost any work you produce. Whether you are writing a paper, making a speech, giving an interview, having an important conversation, or leading and managing your staff, knowing how to think and speak like a debater will help you achieve your desired outcome. However, do not become an argumentative or quarrelsome person just because you want to win every argument.

What is Debate-thinking

Approach every project using the six steps a debater would use to approach a motion.

The thought process behind analysing any project in your daily life or your work is no different from analysing a debate motion. The only major difference is that in a debate, you are assigned a motion and allocated your side. In real life, you must *re-imagine* the project as a debate motion, and then analyse the issue as though you were on a debate team that was arguing for (or against) that motion.

Debate-thinking, therefore, is the mindset that every piece of work you do has a specific goal, and a large part of that goal involves winning over the eventual "audience" for that work. Famous military strategists, businesspeople, politicians, and academics have all promoted variants of this style of thinking, where every problem is approached in a critical and analytical way, a robust solution is developed with all possible opposition pre-empted, and a persuasive "sales pitch" is made to garner support for your idea. In a nutshell: Think, speak, win.

Debate-thinking can be summarised in the same six steps that were covered in Chapter 8, *Putting It All Together*:

Step 1: Define the objective.

Set the context (why is this an important issue now), aim (what is the objective of the debate), definition (key terms), criteria (how do you evaluate which is the best solution), and scope (what issues are within the bounds of this debate). This is covered in detail in Chapter 2, *Defining the Objective*.

Step 2: Build a case.

Identify the stakeholders (who is affected by the topic, who can decide the outcome), settle your case structure (how are you going to organise your case), outline any policy (how will your solution be implemented), and, if required, come up with a memorable caseline. This is covered in detail in Chapter 3.

Step 3: Make logical arguments.

Every argument you make to support your case should follow the Title-Reason-Evidence-Significance (TRES) framework that was covered in Chapter 4, on *Logical Arguments*.

Step 4: Consider rebuttal.

This step has two parts to it. For the first part, you must anticipate how an opposing team would argue their case, and prepare rebuttal for their potential arguments. This is commonly known as "playing the Devil's Advocate" for your own case. For the second part, you must prepare your own rebuttal, to attack the credibility of any opposing arguments (if there are any). Use the structure described in Chapter 5 as a guide.

Step 5: Consider interjections.

The first four steps will establish the content of your project. This fifth step is optional, depending on whether you are expecting to receive any questions midway through your delivery. If your output is a written piece of work, there is no need to consider interjections because it does not apply. However, if you are giving a speech which has time for a Q&A, or if you are delivering a presentation to an audience who might interrupt you with some questions, you should review the guidelines in Chapter 6.

Step 6: Consider style.

The last step is to consider the style of the project, in terms of how it sounds or reads to an audience. If you are producing a written piece of work, style refers to your choice of words, and the accompanying tone, language, structure. If you are delivering the content orally, then you should consider the full range of vocal, visual, and verbal style elements discussed in Chapter 7.

Don't argue for no reason.

A small caution for debaters-to-be though: There is a difference between knowing *how* to debate, and knowing *when* to debate. You do not need to treat every conversation as a debate that you need to win. You must develop the maturity to know when and why to argue – and when you sense that there is no point arguing further, accept it graciously.

Winning an audience can sometimes be done without winning every argument; and conversely, if you doggedly try to win every argument, you might end up losing the audience.

> "*I argue very well. Ask any of my remaining friends. I can win an argument on any topic, against any opponent. People know this, and steer clear of me at parties. Often, as a sign of their great respect, they don't even invite me.*"
>
> — DAVE BARRY

Problem-solving

Problem-solving skills give debaters the upper hand in life.

Aside from persuasion skills, debating gives you the skills to think of solutions to difficult problems facing the world today. When you debate the existence of the death penalty, you have to understand the context of the problem, think about the goals of the death penalty and the justice system as a whole, and discuss the merits and demerits of alternatives, as well as the viability of implementing any other system. This same logical thought process can be adapted from debating and applied to almost any problem that you face in life or work.

Without any structure to help you think of ideas, brainstorming can be very difficult. Most people get stuck and have a "brain-freeze" when asked to brainstorm without any guidance. This can be very easily overcome by applying the Debate-thinking framework, so you will never feel stuck again.

There are open-ended problems and also specific dilemmas.

Open-ended problems are characterised by almost infinite or limitless sets of possible solutions, for example, "What should we do next weekend?" There are countless different ways that you could spend a weekend.

Specific dilemmas are different. They require you to choose between a finite set of specific options. One example of a specific dilemma is, "Should we watch the new James Bond movie next weekend, or should we play basketball?" There are clear options in this dilemma that need to be compared and evaluated against each other.

Debate-thinking works best when you are faced with specific dilemmas, because it is easiest to imagine what the two sides are going to be (in the example above, one side would argue for James

Bond, while the other would argue for basketball). However, Debate-thinking can also be applied to more open-ended problems with a little bit of effort. The 6-step framework for analysing the problem in both cases remains the same.

Re-imagine every problem as a debate motion.

If you are new to debating, the thought processes and methodologies may feel unfamiliar and may not come naturally to you. You should thus start your problem-solving in a systematic way that follows closely the elements of debating, so that the skills in this book can be applied immediately to the problem. This might seem a little artificial at first, but it is a good start, until you become more comfortable with Debate-thinking – and then it will come naturally, without the artificial rigour of these steps.

If you are faced with a specific dilemma to solve, start by rephrasing the dilemma as a debate motion.

> For example, if you are having difficulty deciding which car to buy — a BMW or a Toyota? — you could re-imagine the dilemma as a debate topic: "The Toyota is a better car to buy than the BMW." This would allow the imaginary proposition team to argue in favour of the Toyota, while the imaginary opposition team could argue in favour of the BMW. This is a simple two-sided debate for a specific dilemma.

If you are faced with a more complex open-ended problem, try to change the topic around, or create three or more sides. There are no constraints on the rules of this "debate," because it is purely an imaginary exercise designed to give you some rigour in your problem-solving.

> For example, if you had a more open-ended problem on the same issue above, you could phrase the debate topic as "What is the best

transportation option for my salary?" and then create imaginary teams arguing in turn for buying a Toyota, a BMW, a Honda motorcycle—and even one team to argue, "Don't buy a car, take the bus!" This allows you to rationalise all the possible options.

Step 1: Understand the topic.

What is the aim of the debate?

Once you have come up with the debate topic, think about what you need to do to "win" the debate. Examine whether you need to prove that something is true (is it a fact), what you think should be done (what is your opinion), how you think something should be done (what is your policy or proposal), or what you think will happen in the future (trend and analysis).

For our above example on purchasing a car, it can be thought of as a debate of opinion. Which car should you buy? Why? What is your opinion, and what are the arguments you have to support that opinion?

Alternatively, if you were comparing between two specific cars and needed to discover which was the better car, you could have a debate of fact: Which car is better? What are the facts and arguments that support this claim?

Determine the sides in this "debate."

There are many ways to determine what sides should be debated. One helpful way to think about this is to remember who the stakeholders are in the decision. If your decision about which car to buy has an impact on your family, your friends, your colleagues, and yourself, then you could split up the debate by those groupings. That is, one team would argue from the family's perspective, another team your friends' perspective, another your colleagues', and so on.

Each team would recommend which car you should buy based on what they think is in their own best interests. It would obviously be beneficial if you could get the actual stakeholders involved and get them to debate from their own perspectives so that you can hear all views and come to the best decision.

If you are brainstorming in a group or office setting, you could split the group into a few teams and assign different perspectives to each team, then let each team come up with their own case. This would help ensure that every view is given an equal airing. You can either let people choose their teams (that is, they have a natural preference for Toyotas or BMWs) or assign them.

> *"In debate, [a person] randomly was assigned to one side or the other. This had at least one virtue – it made [the person] see that there was more than one side to these complex issues."*
>
> — JOSEPH E. STIGLITZ

Follow Step 2 (Build a case) and Step 3 (Make logical arguments) to develop the content for your case.

Apply the framework in this book to each side of the case. Define the topic and the key terms; define your criteria to evaluate the various cases; develop a case for each side; and think of a few key logical arguments (with the proper reasoning and evidence to support them). If you do this for each side, you will have successfully brainstormed multiple solutions to the problem, and you will have more clarity on what should be done.

Motion: A Toyota is a better car for me than a BMW.

- Sides: Team Toyota and Team BMW
- Criteria: (1) Quality of the car (reliability, servicing, engine performance, sound system, etc.); (2) Long-term cost of the car (purchase price, servicing costs, fuel consumption, etc.)
- Team Toyota would have to come up with a good case and arguments as to why this is true.
- Team BMW would have to refute the Toyota case and come up with their own case and arguments to explain why the BMW is a better car for you.

Step 4: Consider rebuttal, to make your case more robust.

Most people are satisfied once they come up with a few decent arguments for their case. Not debaters. Debate-thinking encourages you to find the possible flaws and loopholes in the arguments, to ensure that they stand up to scrutiny. You can use the rebuttal as "feedback" to iteratively improve your proposal or solution. This means your case will be more robust as a result of the rebuttal.

You can either pre-empt rebuttal from the other "side" and thereby strengthen your own case, or you can hold an actual debate or discussion to get external rebuttal for your case.

Rebuttal from Team BMW: "You claimed that prestige was not important to you in your choice of car — but the fact that you care about what other people think about your choice of car implies that prestige is indeed a factor. BMWs are more prestigious than Toyotas, and will impress people more."

You can use this rebuttal from Team BMW to change or strengthen your arguments for Team Toyota: "I do care what other people think about my choice of car, but I am not trying to impress them with how glamorous my car is. I want them to approve of my car choice because it is practical and affordable in the long run. In this aspect,

Toyota is more practical and affordable, and will win their approval."

In the end, you would have arrived at better arguments to support your proposal to buy a Toyota. Alternatively, if team BMW manages to convince you that a BMW is better, you can take confidence in knowing that the decision was a very well-considered one.

Debate-thinking helps you come up with better solutions to any problem.

For problem-solving, Steps 5 and 6 of the Debate-thinking framework – that is, interjections and style – are not really necessary. Debate-thinking gives you a solid framework to analyse any problem small or large. The example in this section about buying a car may seem rather trivial, but the methodology can be extended to problems of much more serious nature. It is always better to approach a problem using a simple framework that leads to robust solutions. Whether it is an actual debate or purely an intellectual exercise, you must follow the rigour of Debate-thinking in order to reap results.

Writings

Written output forms a very large part of our school, work, and even personal life. We are required to write academic essays, work-related policy papers or proposals, and we often have to write personal emails or blog articles as well. All of these can be done better by using Debate-thinking.

Re-imagine the writing assignment as a debate topic.

Written assignments are often very similar to debate topics. You should thus have no trouble rephrasing the topic to be more like a debate topic, so that you can analyse the issue from a Debate-thinking perspective.

Step 1: Understand the topic and the aim of the "debate."

Just like in a debate, you must understand what you need to prove in order to "win" with your piece of writing.

An *informational report* that updates people about something is very similar to a "Debate of Fact," because you are explaining to your readers what the facts of a situation are.

A financial report for a company can be easily re-imagined as a debate of fact: "Company ABC is doing financially well this year." Your objective is thus to convince readers using logical arguments that the motion is true. Your arguments will need to be based on sound reasons (for example, why will your current strategy work best in the future economic environment), and evidence (what does your balance sheet look like this year).

An *issue analysis* or *assessment paper* is closer to a "Debate of Opinion" or a "Debate of Trend and Analysis," because you must provide your views and opinions on the issue – whether personal or official – supported by evidence.

An essay on the political dynamic between China and the U.S. could be re-imagined as a Debate of Opinion: "Relations between China and the U.S. are deteriorating significantly"; or as a Debate of Trend and Analysis: "China and the U.S. will go to war by 2020." Your key claim is the debate topic itself, and you must spend the entire essay convincing people of your assessment, analysis, and opinion.

Similarly, an office paper discussing a potential merger with Company X could be re-imagined as a Debate of Opinion: "Merging with X will be beneficial for our Company A." Again, you must now persuade the reader that the topic is true using Debate-thinking.

Finally, if you are writing a document that seeks the approval of a board to pursue a certain proposal, you are engaging in a "Debate of Policy" because you must not only convince the readers that something should be done, you also have to explain to them how you propose for it to be done.

> If your company is considering a merger with Company XYZ, and you are trying to convince the readers that it will bring benefits to your company, you can imagine the issue as a Debate of Policy. You must first convince the reader that the merger is a good thing, and then propose a specific form for the merger, a policy proposal that can be approved by a Board of Directors or Chairman.

Complete Steps 1, 2, 3 and 4 to develop your content.

Once you have completed your preparation for the content of your report, you are ready to start actually writing the report. Since written documents have no interjections, you can skip Step 5.

Step 6: Consider style.

Written style is different from spoken style.

The style of a written document is very different from the style of a debate speech, or any oral presentation. When you speak to an audience, you can use your body, face, and voice to convey importance, irony, sarcasm, and many other tones. Since a written document cannot capture vocal changes and facial expressions, these elements are lost. Thus, the style of writing a document must be very different from the style of presenting a speech.

Pick a style that works for your intended audience.

If you are writing a blog article or an email to a colleague, you can use a casual or even colloquial tone. However, if you are writing an essay or a paper that will be assessed by a teacher or a boss, a casual tone may not work.

Use short sentences and simple words if possible.

Using uncommon and very long words just to show off that you have a large vocabulary is not a good idea because you may alienate some readers, who don't understand the word, or may not appreciate your showing off. Short sentences are easier to read, and easier to comprehend. Many readers are unable to digest very long sentences that are tenuously held together by "but," "and," "therefore," and other such conjunctions. Make each concept into its own sentence if possible, rather than stringing many concepts into one long sentence.

Speeches and presentations

Many people are afraid of giving speeches, and thus try to avoid it. Hopefully this book has changed that. If you are asked to deliver a speech at an event, or if suddenly somebody in your office thrusts the microphone in front of your face and expects you to give a short speech, this section should help you immensely.

Prepared speeches — follow the full framework.

Step 1: Understand the topic.

Every speech has an objective. If you are asked to give a speech at an event, talk to the organisers to find out if they have any specific requests for your speech's objectives. Some speeches require you to convince an audience of your point of view, or at least to inform them of your perspective. Even for speeches that seem not to have any overt objective, there is still a hidden objective: You are trying to build a connection and establish rapport with the audience. The difference between debating and giving speeches, though, is that in a debate, it is acceptable to state clearly what your objective is, whereas in a speech, it would sound very odd if you openly stated what your objective was. Imagine if your boss came up and said, "Good evening! I would like to speak to you tonight to build rapport with my audience!"

Step 2: Build a case.

In a debate, you have to identify the stakeholders and analyse the issue from their perspectives. What are their motivations, and what are they looking out for? In a speech, the stakeholders are your audience – both the live audience as well as the ones who might be reading the speech in the newspapers or company magazine. Think about the issue from their perspectives: What do they want to know about it, and what can you tell them to help achieve your objective?

Steps 3 and 4: Make logical arguments and consider rebuttal.

Once you are clear about your desired objectives and the case, the next steps are to finish the content for your speech by making compelling logical arguments and considering the relevant rebuttal.

You will rarely have to answer questions in the middle of a speech, so we can skip Step 5 (Interjections) for now. If there is a Question-and-Answer session after your speech, you may want to read the next section on interviews.

Step 6: Consider style.

In a speech, there is a lot of room for you to play with the style of delivery. This includes using innovative introductions and conclusions, humour, and many other rhetorical devices that we have discussed. Since the speech will be a rehearsed and prepared one, you can memorise the style and delivery of key points in your speech.

Impromptu speeches — use a simplified framework.

Even among people who are not afraid of public speaking, most of them are still a little nervous when asked to give a speech without warning or prior notice. Debaters have the upper hand here, because they are used to situations in which they have very little time to prepare their content for a speech, and many times they have to react "on the fly" to changes in their opponents' cases or difficult interjections. As soon as you are asked to give an impromptu speech, take a few seconds to think through the following condensed framework:

Step 1: Quickly understand the topic — what is the objective?
Do you just want to share your opinion on the issue at hand? Do you want to build a relationship with the audience? Do you want to disagree with the previous speaker? Pick just one simple objective that you think fits the expectations of the audience or the person who has asked you to speak.

Steps 2, 3 and 4: Quickly outline just one key argument that would support this objective.
Do not bother trying to develop a robust case if you don't have time. Jump straight in with one argument that has the bare essentials. State your point, give a reason, give an example, and conclude. You won't have time to research, so your example could be a simple story from your experience or funny anecdote that supports the point you are making. Even though this may not be an excellent speech, it is better than freezing up in front of the audience or mumbling something incoherent or sounding stupid. You will emerge from the experience relatively unscathed, which is much better than if you did not have any framework to prepare your content quickly.

Step 6: Keep the style simple — focus on a good introduction and simple conclusion.

As long as you speak with confidence, people will be impressed because most people realise that you are giving this speech with no preparation. Focus on having a good introduction that establishes a connection and builds rapport with the audience. You can make a joke about being thrust into the spot and use humour to defuse the tension for yourself. Once you have made your short speech, wrap up quickly and confidently. Don't fade off meekly. If you have a strong presence on stage, people will remember your speech positively.

Interviews and Q&As

There are many situations in which you are required to answer difficult questions without any external assistance. Whether it is a job interview, a scholarship interview, or a Q&A session at the end of a speech, these are often stressful experiences for people. Luckily, debaters are trained to handle difficult interjections. Those same skills can be applied to these situations. Since you will not have to present a full speech in these situations, we will jump straight to Steps 4 and 5 in the Debate-thinking framework. Nonetheless, there is still some value in going through Steps 1, 2 and 3 just to ensure that you know the objective of the interview session (to get a job, to get a scholarship), and that everything you say builds towards that objective.

Step 4: Consider rebuttal.

Prepare yourself before the interview or the Q&A session by thinking of potential questions that you will receive. For example, if you are at a scholarship interview and you need to convince the panel that you are a deserving candidate, you may want to look through your resume and see if there are any gaps or weak areas, and think of how you can explain these to the panel. If you have stellar grades but you never played a sport in your life, you should anticipate a question along these lines and think of answers in advance.

Step 5: Consider interjections.

Re-read the section in Chapter 6 on "Responding to an interjection" to understand how to handle difficult questions. In summary, listen carefully to the key words in the question to understand the intent of the question. Paraphrase the question if you need to either defuse the negativity in the question or to stall for time. Respond to the issue at the heart of the interjection head-on. End your response on a positive note – a "counter-attack" of sorts. The following example should make this a little clearer.

> Interviewer: "It is clear from your school record that you were a nerd, because your grades are exceptional but you never played any sports. We prefer well-rounded students, and you are not one of them. Do you agree?"
>
> This question is very negative (possibly more so than you would encounter in real life, but it is a useful example to learn from).
>
> Key words in the question: No sports = not well-rounded.
>
> Defuse the negativity in the question first: "It's true; I didn't play any sports in high school because I found other passions to pursue. But that does not mean that I am not well-rounded, because sports are not the only way to make a person well-rounded."
>
> Respond to the heart of the interjection: "I didn't play any sports because I found my passion elsewhere, doing volunteer work at an elderly home. This demanded a lot of time from me on weekdays after school and even some weekends, so I didn't have time to pursue

sports. I also did not think it was necessary to pursue sports in order to become a well-rounded person because I learned all the same traits and habits in my volunteering work. For example, I learned about leadership and teamwork when I was in charge of a group of younger volunteers...." Add more stories here about skills you learned that are normally associated with sportsmen only.

Conclude on a counter-attack: "In fact, I think I am more well-rounded than many sportsmen because I also learned compassion and charity, which is rare among sportsmen because they may not have many opportunities to lend others a helping hand, because of the highly competitive nature of sports."

You have thus taken a very negative question, defused it, responded to the core issue, and even turned it around to make their case seem weak.

Step 6: Consider style.

Again, think about the qualities that the panel would like to see in a potential candidate, and try and embody that with your style. If you are a nervous wreck, getting all the answers spot-on will still not suffice because the panel will not want to give a job or scholarship to somebody who looks so nervous. They would rather see you speak with confidence and remain calm even in the face of difficult questions.

Leadership and management

Every book on leadership and management has a chapter on persuasive communication skills.

A successful leader and manager must be able to motivate his staff to perform at their very best, in order for the team to succeed. Having impressive plans, strategies, and goals is useless without the ability to convince people to follow you. Persuasive communication is thus at the heart of good leadership and management. Debating is all about persuasive communication.

Teams work best when they understand your message clearly.

When you send an email or deliver a speech to your office, they must be able to walk away from the speech with a clear sense of purpose and priorities. You must "win" the hearts and minds of your staff, because every time you "lose" or fail to win them over, your authority and credibility as a leader diminishes. If your speech or email is incoherent, unstructured, overly rambling, or difficult for them to understand, you lose. If they are not convinced of the need to pursue your proposal or have doubts about the validity of some of your arguments, you lose. If they don't sense your charisma and confidence in the speech, you lose.

Miscommunications can be disastrous in a leadership context. An unclear speech or email can result in wasted hours of work, or even the failure of a project. If an email contains an ambiguous instruction, your staff may accidentally do the wrong thing. Be clear and thorough by sticking to Debate-thinking.

Modern workers prefer to be convinced, not ordered.

This is especially true for younger staff in their late 20s and 30s, who do not take kindly to being "bossed around," even if you are their boss. Leadership books espouse the virtue of infusing your staff with a sense of purpose, so that they understand and appreciate the goals of the team and are self-motivated to help the team achieve those goals. Forcing them to achieve the goals using the traditional carrot-and-stick (that is, raising their pay, or firing them) will work only for a few of them, and only in the short term. In order to truly infuse your staff with purpose, you must convince them.

Using the Debate-thinking framework, persuade them of the

importance of the goal and how their efforts help to achieve it. If they have doubts, allow them to ask questions. Deal with their questions – even the very negative ones – using the steps covered in the earlier section. Let them feel comfortable asking questions, and give them good answers. You will be surprised by how hard and intelligently people are willing to work when they believe in the importance of their job, and especially so if they have confidence in you as a leader.

Use Debate-thinking to get the best ideas from your staff.

Many workers often feel uncomfortable sharing their ideas and views in the office, because of their inexperience or personality. This hampers the free flow of ideas, and may result in your office culture being dominated by a few talkative workers. If you put everybody (including the quiet ones) into a healthy debate setting and assign people different perspectives to debate on a particular issue, they will have no choice but to brainstorm and generate arguments. This will help the quiet ones to open up, because they feel less exposed (they are taking a contrary view because it is part of the exercise, not because they "dare to go against the other staff.") It is also a great team-building exercise to get people talking about new issues or proposals.

Force opposing views to develop more robust proposals and to avoid the danger of "group-think."

When a new idea or proposal is discussed, people may feel uncomfortable disagreeing with the proposal or making drastic changes to the initial proposal. They might be afraid of being labelled as "not team players" because they went against the grain. This is unhealthy, because it means that potentially bad ideas might get approved because nobody was daring enough to point out the flaws. Pit your staff into a hypothetical debate – with some staff assigned to "defend" the proposal, and some to "attack" the proposal – and you will get a more thorough discussion of the merits and demerits of the idea. You can then use all the points to strengthen or change the proposal and make it better.

Sometimes all the staff in an office "think" in the same way (perhaps as a result of the recruitment or training). This might sound wonderful, but it can cause "group-think," where the group is unable to think independently and discover the merits and demerits from their own perspective. This means that flaws or weaknesses in an idea might not get exposed. You can break this cycle by deliberately pitting the staff into the same imaginary debate above.

Apply Debate-thinking to your own work and teach your staff how to apply it to their work.

If your whole team is able to communicate clearly and convincingly, time will not be wasted trying to get the message across. Your time will be better spent actually achieving the objectives – a much more productive way to work.

SUMMARY

1: What is Debate

Topic

- A topic is required to focus the debate.
- Topics must be controversial.
- Topics can be from current affairs or philosophical dilemmas.

Debaters

- Debaters are placed into teams, for and against the topic.
- Debaters then argue for their assigned side.

Format and structure

- A pre-agreed set of rules allows the debate to proceed smoothly.
- At least two sides are needed – one side for the topic and one side against the topic (Proposition versus Opposition, or Government versus Opposition).
- Debates are usually judged, and a winner is selected.

2: Defining the Objective

Set the context

- Background research and current affairs are important to understand why the topic is being debated now.

Define the objective

- Keep your definition clear, simple, and based on a "reasonable" person's interpretation.
- Don't rely on dictionaries alone.

What is the aim of the debate?

- Do you need to show *why* something should be done, *how* something should be done, or both?
- Is it a debate of fact, opinion, policy, or trend?

Evaluation criteria

- Develop a thorough and fair set of criteria to evaluate both teams' cases.
- Explain how to measure the "subjective" elements or words in the topic.

Set the scope

- Narrow or broaden the scope to suit the motion, if the rules allow you to do so.

Avoid unfair definitions

- Avoid definitions that are biased, circular, loaded, or unfairly scoped.
- Use terms consistently across your team.

3: Building A Case

Identify the stakeholders

- There are two main groups of stakeholders: those who are affected by the outcome of the topic, and those who can control the outcome of the topic.
- Analyse the incentives and responsibilities of each stakeholder.

Structure a case

- The case should be structured in a way that is simple and thorough, covering all aspects of what your side needs to prove in order to win.

Create a case-line

- The team should have a case slogan that is memorable, simple, and covers your whole case.

Propose a course of action

- Establish clearly what is the problem identified by the motion.
- State the evaluation criteria for your solution.
- Explain the mechanics of your solution.

4: Logical Arguments

Title

- Introduce each argument with a title that is clear, directly related to the topic, and memorable.

Reason

- Analyse the logic and rationale behind the argument, and give a theoretical framework for the point.

Evidence

- Support your argument with examples, analogies, studies, data, and other forms of substantiation.

Significance

- Explain how this point links back to your team's case and how it helps to prove or disprove the motion.

5: Rebuttal

Listening and understanding

- Listen for key words and concepts from the other side, as well as for important things they did not say.

Finding and analysing the flaws

- Rebuttal should prove that the other team's argument is not true, or, even if it is true, not significant.
- The priority of rebuttal should be (1) definitions and scope, (2) team case and major arguments, (3) specific important points, and (4) only if necessary, examples. This is the same priority in which you should defend any attacks against your case.

Rebutting definitions

- Only rebut definitions if they are unfair or you have a better definition to offer.

Rebutting arguments

- Are the grounds or premises for their point valid?
- Is their logic and reasoning correct?
- Is their evidence sufficient?
- Is their conclusion correct, and is it significant?

Defending your case

- Rebut their rebuttal, and then counter-attack.

Preparing rebuttals

- Prepare evidence and arguments to rebut the other team's expected case.

6: Interjections

What is an interjection

- Interjections are condensed rebuttals offered in the middle of an opponent's speech in order to reduce the persuasiveness of their argument.

Offering interjections

- Zoom in on a single flaw and attack it.
- You can use the "Statement then question" format or design your own interjection, as long as it is concise.

Responding to interjections

- Listen for the key words and issues in the interjection.
- Paraphrase the interjection if you need to defuse the negative tone or to give yourself time to think of a response.
- Always counter-attack once you have responded to the interjection. Never end on a defensive tone.

7: Style

Visual style

- Present a positive image of yourself on stage, through your posture, gestures, and attire.
- Make good eye contact.

Vocal style

- Control your volume, speed and pace so that the audience can understand your speech.
- Train your tone and timbre to achieve a more credible public speaking voice.
- Vary your vocal delivery to differentiate between more important and less important points.

Verbal style

- Use simple language.
- Avoid meaningless fillers ("Ladies and Gentlemen").
- Experiment with repetition, alliteration, quotes, metaphors and similes.

Personal style

- Practise in front of a mirror or video-record yourself to understand your personal style.
- Learn positive traits from others.

Winning over the audience

- Start with a strong introduction; end with a memorable conclusion.
- Be earnest, humble, personal, polite, funny, charming, and inspirational.

8: Putting It All Together

Impromptu debates

- Step 1: Individual Brainstorming (5 mins)
- Step 2: Define the topic and the team's objective (10 mins)
- Step 3: Build the team case and anticipate the other team's case (15 mins)
- Step 4: Develop your own arguments individually (20 mins)
- Step 5: Regroup and share (and rehearse) (10 mins)

Teamwork on the floor

- Work closely with your team-mates by sharing knowledge, examples, rebuttals; do not be selfish.
- Do not undermine your team-mates.

9: Coaching and Teaching

Selecting a debate team

- Have open auditions or hold intra-school debates to pick your school team.
- Select a variety of speakers and enough members for two teams (to spar).

Training foundation skills

- Play specific games and activities to build up competency in individual skills.

Team training

- Sparring sessions are the best training. Coaches should come prepared with the motion, speaker positions, and should have researched the motion already to counter-check the students' arguments.
- Debrief the students thoroughly starting with the big issues and then going to individual pointers.
- Be specific and clear in your advice.

Debate in the classroom

- Introduce debate into the classroom progressively, as students may be less confident and articulate than debaters until they have learned the proper skills.

Coaching philosophy

- Being positive and supportive is more effective than being mean.
- Do not bring your personal beliefs and aversions into the topics.

10: Judging

The role of the judge

- A judge (or panel of judges) picks the winner of the debate based on the quality of the debaters, not their personal feelings on the topic.
- Judges sometimes score the speakers/teams.
- Judges sometimes deliver the verdict.

Philosophies of judging

- The philosophy of judging is dependent on the format of debate.
- Judges can be a blank slate, a next opponent speaker, or a rational, intelligent man on the street.

Preparation before the debate

- Be familiar with the rules, format, scoring criteria.
- Know at least as much about the topic as the "man on the street."

Judging a debate

- Listen closely and analyse what is being said.
- Avoid bringing in your personal biases.
- Cross-check your scores.

Delivering a verdict

- Give a short, precise, positive speech that captures the key points of the debate as seen by the judges.

Common mistakes

- Don't be mean, unprofessional, disrespectful, arrogant.

11: Applying Debate-Thinking Every Day

The 6 steps of Debate-Thinking

- Step 1: Define the Objective
- Step 2: Build a Case
- Step 3: Make Logical Arguments
- Step 4: Consider Rebuttal
- Step 5: Consider Interjections
- Step 6: Consider Style

Appendix 1

COMMON DEBATE FORMATS

World Schools Debating Championships

The most common high-school debating formats in the world today are based on the WSDC rules.

The WSDC has been held annually in different cities around the world since 1988. The 2010 competition was held in Qatar, and attracted teams from 57 countries, making it the largest international high-school debate competition. Owing to its long history and global prevalence, the WSDC format has been adopted by most countries for their own local competitions. Singapore, the U.K., Australia, and many other countries use the WSDC format. The website for the WSDC contains the full rules and guides (www.schoolsdebate.com).

Every WSDC debate has a specific debate topic — the motion.

There are many ways to phrase the motion. Some countries like to use simple direct English: "We should abolish the death penalty." Some countries prefer to phrase it as though the students were debating in the British House of Lords or Commons (which is where the debate format originated): "This house believes that we should abolish the death penalty." The issue to be debated is the same.

WSDC topics are clear and specific, and try to avoid ambiguity in the phrasing so that both teams know exactly what the issue to be debated is. A clear and specific debate topic is like the one given above. By contrast, a vague debate topic would be something like "Bigger is better." It is not clear in this topic exactly what the two teams should be debating, and it could result in confusion – what does "bigger" refer to (Body size? Government?). WSDC generally avoids such vague topics.

Students can be given the topic a few days in advance, or just an hour before.

Debates in which the motions are given in advance are known as *prepared debates*, because students have time to research thoroughly and prepare sufficiently. Debates in which the motions are given just a short while before the debate (usually an hour in advance) are known as *impromptu debates*. Impromptu debates are very challenging, because students must come up with their case and speeches without the benefit of detailed research. They are usually not allowed to refer to the internet or bring in extensive reading material to help them prepare their case, and teams are isolated from their coaches and teachers so that they cannot ask them for help. This is to ensure that the teams are tested for their own abilities and knowledge, without any external assistance.

There are two teams: The Proposition and the Opposition.

The Proposition argues in favour of the motion; it supports the topic as it is phrased. In the earlier example topic on abolishing the death penalty, the Proposition is the team that argues that the death penalty *should* be abolished. In some countries, the Proposition is referred to as the "Government," again in reference to the roots of this debate format, but the roles of the team are the same.

Sometimes, but very rarely, the Proposition team is called the "Positive" or "Affirmative" team.

The Opposition is the other team, and it argues against the motion and against the other team, that the death penalty should *not* be abolished.

Each team has three speakers.

There are three Proposition speakers, known as the "First Proposition," "Second Proposition," and "Third Proposition" respectively. Likewise, the Opposition also has three speakers, known as the "First Opposition," "Second Opposition," and "Third Opposition."

Regardless of what the country chooses to call the Proposition and Opposition teams, the speaker names, roles, and speaking order remain pretty much the same. Each speaker has a fixed amount of time to deliver their speech, usually between five to eight minutes, depending on the skill level of competition – debates featuring inexperienced or young debaters tend to have five-minute speeches, while the international WSDC debates feature eight-minute speeches. The two teams alternate their speaking turns thus:

1. The First Proposition opens the debate by introducing the topic, providing definitions, and starting their team's case.
2. The First Opposition goes next, to rebut what the Proposition team has argued and to start the Opposition's team case.
3. The Second Proposition speaker then continues the Proposition's case and rebuts the Opposition speaker before him.
4. The Second Opposition speaker continues the Opposition case and rebuts the Proposition case thus far.
5. The Third Proposition rebuts the Opposition case thus far.
6. The Third Opposition then rebuts the Proposition case.

After all three speakers have had their turn giving a speech, both teams are given a final speech to summarise the debate and their case. This final speech is referred to as a "summary," "closing," or "reply" speech (probably because you are "replying" to the other team at the end of the debate). This speech is half the duration of a normal speech – that is, it lasts around three to four minutes. The speech is given by either the First or Second speaker of the team (so one of those speakers will have to speak twice during the debate). These rules are also varied slightly depending on the skill level of the competition. For the "Summary" speech, the speaking order is reversed, so the Proposition speaks at the very end instead of right after the Third Opposition.

7. The Opposition Summary speech (which can be given by either the First or Second Opposition) closes the case for the Opposition.
8. The Proposition Summary speech (which is likewise delivered by either the First or Second Proposition) closes the case for the Proposition.

Debaters from the other team are allowed to offer short interjections called "Points of Information" (POI).

The speaker on the stage (that is, the debater whose turn it is currently to speak) may choose to accept or reject the POI when it is offered by the other team's debater. Generally, it is considered bad form for a speaker to reject all the POIs, because it indicates that the speaker may not be confident enough to accept an interjection.

WSDC speakers are judged on Content, Style, and Strategy.

Judges in WSDC use a marking sheet to evaluate the performance of each debater, and cumulatively, the performance of the teams. Each debater is scored out of 100 marks, with 40 marks for Content (the actual substance and matter of your case), 40 marks for Style (how

ABC Debate Competition: Adjudicator's Score-sheet

Room: ________ Division: ______ Round: ______ Date: __________

Motion

Proposition:

Name	Style	Content	Strategy	Total	Comments
First speaker	/40	/40	/20	/100	
Second speaker	/40	/40	/20	/100	
Third speaker	/40	/40	/20	/100	
Reply speaker	/20	/20	/10	/50	
				/350	

Opposition:

Name	Style	Content	Strategy	Total	Comments
First speaker	/40	/40	/20	/100	
Second speaker	/40	/40	/20	/100	
Third speaker	/40	/40	/20	/100	
Reply speaker	/20	/20	/10	/50	
				/350	

Winning team:

Rationale for decision

Adjudicator's name: ______________ Signature: _________________

the arguments are delivered to the audience) and 20 marks for Strategy (how cleverly the debater utilised the techniques and tactics of debating). The First, Second and Third speakers of the Proposition and Opposition are all scored out of 100 marks. The reply speech, however, is scored out of 50 marks, because it is a shorter speech. The cumulative score of the three speakers and the reply speech is compared, and the team with the higher score is the winner. Of course, this is a vast over-simplification of the process and goals of adjudication. The facing page includes a sample score-sheet from the debate competition format used in Singapore, which is closely based on the WSDC format. There is a minor difference between this score-sheet and the WSDC official score-sheet though: In the latter, judges can assess the quality of Points of Information (interjections) offered by that speaker and award or deduct two points from the speaker's overall score based on their POIs.

British Parliamentary format

The principles of the British Parliamentary (BP) format are generally consistent with WSDC, and most debaters are thus fairly comfortable alternating between the two formats.

BP debates, unlike WSDC, have two teams per side.

The biggest difference between WSDC and the BP format is that the BP format features four teams: two teams on the Proposition, and two teams on the Opposition. This is a direct evolution from the historic British Parliament, which featured a coalition Government (that is, one made up of two separate factions or teams) and a coalition Opposition (likewise, made up of two separate factions or teams). The teams were referred to as the Opening Government, the Closing Government, the Opening Opposition, and the Closing

Opposition. Each of these four teams had two speakers each. Thus, there were eight speakers during a BP debate, as compared to only six speakers in a WSDC debate.

Only one team of the four could win the debate, so even the two teams on the same side would have to prove to the Judges that they were superior to the other team on their side. That is, the Opening Government would have to beat the Opening and Closing Opposition, and they would also have to prove that they were better than the Closing Government team. Because of the complexity of this format, it is usually only used for advanced debate competitions.

Other debate formats

This book does not cover the details and specific rules and formats of all the different types of debating in the world. There are too many to mention, and they are constantly evolving. Many countries also have their own debating formats.

American debating formats

The U.S. has its own unique formats like "Karl Popper," "Lincoln Douglas," and "National Forensics League," but these formats are almost never used outside the country. Most international debaters find these American formats highly technical and too complex for a general audience to follow without prior training in that format. Detailed explanations of these formats (and many more) can be found online.

Appendix 2

SAMPLE DEBATE TOPICS

Compiling an exhaustive list of debate topics will always be impossible – new topics emerge on a daily basis, and event-specific topics quickly become outdated. This appendix lists motions that have been debated in Singapore at the major competitions supported by the Debate Association (Singapore). Take note that the categories into which the motions have been divided should not be used as an indication of how to approach the debate – that is, just because a topic falls under "Economics" does not mean that you should avoid discussing societal or cultural implications.

Practise debating the topics using the steps in this book, and you will be well on your way to becoming a great debater who can think faster, speak better, and win audiences.

Economics

1. We believe in a legislated minimum wage.
2. We believe that alcohol and tobacco companies should not be allowed to advertise their products.
3. We believe that China's position as the world's factory does more harm than good.
4. We believe that fast food companies should pay compensation for damaging people's health.
5. We believe that globalisation perpetuates social inequality.
6. We believe that governments should always bail out big companies.
7. We believe that the use of foreign workers has done more harm than good.
8. We would ban the advertising of fast food.
9. We would disallow foreign investment in domestic utilities and telecommunication entities.
10. We would have the First World forgive Third World debt.
11. We would impose a tax on large bonuses paid to bankers.
12. We would increase income tax and not the Goods & Services Tax.
13. We would keep trade and environment separate.
14. We would make environmental protection a condition for receiving developmental aid.
15. We would nationalise all natural resources in the developing world.
16. We would not reduce taxes during an economic recession.

Laws and Society

1. We believe that acts of civil disobedience are justifiable.
2. We believe that adultery should be criminalised.
3. We believe that casinos should not hire former youth offenders.
4. We believe that doctors should be allowed to help terminally-ill patients end their lives.
5. We believe that governments in the developing world should ban sex tourism.
6. We believe that harsh punishments are the best way to deal with juvenile crime.
7. We believe that national security should take precedence over individual rights.
8. We believe that parents should be required to attend compulsory parenting classes.
9. We believe that the sale of human organs should be legalised.
10. We support the imposition of a mandatory night-time curfew on children and teenagers.
11. We support the use of home detention schemes for convicted criminals.
12. We would abolish the death sentence.
13. We would allow any non-criminal to run for office in Singapore.
14. We would ban cosmetic surgery.
15. We would ban gambling on sports events.
16. We would ban private cars from entering the central areas of all major cities.
17. We would ban smoking in all public places.

18. We would ban TV advertisements aimed at children.
19. We would ban video games that depict violence.
20. We would compel journalists to reveal their sources.
21. We would compromise privacy in the interests of national security.
22. We would deny convicted criminals the right to vote.
23. We would lower the voting age in national elections to 16.
24. We would make community service an alternative form of national service.
25. We would make the age of consent relative to the parties involved.
26. We would not allow criminals to profit from their stories.
27. We would not allow religious political parties to stand in elections.
28. We would place quotas on the number of women in elected office.
29. We would prevent the media from reporting on the private lives of politicians.
30. We would prosecute teenagers as adults for criminal offences.
31. We would punish parents for crimes committed by their children.
32. We would remove politicians' immunity from prosecution.
33. We would televise criminal trials.
34. We would use affirmative action in response to historical injustices.

Education and School

1. We believe that academic scholarships should only be given to students who are in financial need.
2. We believe that all secondary schools should be single-sex schools.
3. We believe that all students in secondary and pre-university education should study an equal balance of arts and science subjects.
4. We believe that all students should be required to do compulsory charity work.
5. We believe that higher education should be funded by a graduate tax system.
6. We believe that music, art and drama should be compulsory elements of the curriculum in secondary education.
7. We believe that schools should factor performance at part-time jobs into students' grades.
8. We believe that schools should prohibit their students from creating their own blog websites.
9. We believe that schools should teach abstinence only.
10. We believe that secondary schools should be allowed to set their own curriculum.
11. We believe that Singapore's education system breeds elitism.
12. We believe that the integrated programme school system creates more harm than good.
13. We would abolish all inter-school debating competitions.
14. We would abolish single-sex schools.
15. We would allow hate speech on campuses.
16. We would allow home schooling.

17. We would make secondary schools sell condoms.
18. We would make sex and race quotas compulsory in all tertiary institutes.
19. We would remove all education subsidies for non-citizens.
20. We would remove the compulsory mother tongue requirement in schools.

Politics and International Affairs

1. We believe that America should be the global policeman.
2. We believe that ASEAN has failed.
3. We believe that captured terrorists should be treated as prisoners of war.
4. We believe that democracy is the best system of government for every nation.
5. We believe that disaster relief is better provided by non-governmental organisations than national governments.
6. We believe that formal debates between candidates should be an integral part of all election campaigns.
7. We believe that International Humanitarian Law fails to protect those who need it most.
8. We believe that monarchies should have no place in today's world.
9. We believe that political parties should be allowed to advertise.
10. We believe that politicians should only be allowed to serve in office for a limited period of time.
11. We believe that soldiers who contravene the Geneva Conventions on direct orders should not be liable for their crimes.

12. We believe that the 2003 invasion of Iraq can be justified on humanitarian grounds.
13. We believe that the private lives of public figures should be open to public scrutiny.
14. We believe that the UN needs its own standing army.
15. We believe that the United Nations should take a stronger stand against human rights abuses.
16. We believe that the United States should not withdraw troops from Iraq.
17. We believe that the War on Terror has been counter-productive.
18. We believe that voting in national elections should be compulsory.
19. We believe that wealthy nations should be obliged to accept more refugees.
20. We regret that Obama won the Nobel Peace Prize.
21. We welcome the 44th President of the U.S.A.
22. We would abolish the veto vote in the UN.
23. We would boycott the Beijing Olympics.
24. We would close Guantanamo Bay.
25. We would grant permanent residence to all illegal aliens.
26. We would have ASEAN impose sanctions on Indonesia for the haze.
27. We would impose democracy on developing nations.
28. We would negotiate with terrorists.
29. We would partition Iraq.
30. We would require UN Security Council members to always offer humanitarian aid.

Science and Technology

1. We believe that Facebook and other social networking sites should only be open to individuals aged 16 and above.
2. We believe that Google should be allowed to digitally archive all books.
3. We believe that governments should be allowed to censor the internet.
4. We believe that it's your own fault if others mooch off your unprotected wireless network.
5. We believe that piracy represents a serious threat to the future of the entertainment industry.
6. We believe that science and technology are progressing at a rate too fast for the good of society.
7. We believe that the widespread availability of the internet has brought more harm than good.
8. We would allow all states to use nuclear technology.
9. We would ban all experimentation into animal cloning.
10. We would ban genetically-modified foods.
11. We would disallow anonymity online.
12. We would hand control of the internet to the United Nations.
13. We would legalise stem cell research for therapeutic purposes.

Sports, Arts and Culture

1. We believe that all forms of art should not be subjected to censorship.
2. We believe that cartoons are a negative influence on young children.

3. We believe that cultural treasures belong at home.
4. We believe that elite sportsmen should receive government funding.
5. We believe that fairy tales are a negative influence on young children.
6. We believe that Hollywood has an unhealthy influence on the rest of the world.
7. We believe that hosting the Olympics is not worthwhile.
8. We believe that international sporting events are a waste of money.
9. We believe that national sports leagues should not impose limits on the number of foreign players a team may field.
10. We believe that only local-born citizens should be allowed to represent their country in international sports *(you can replace "international sports" with "Olympics" or "Youth Olympics").*
11. We believe that professional sports players should have salary caps.
12. We believe that sports and politics are a toxic combination.
13. We believe that sportsmen caught taking performance-enhancing drugs should be banned for life.
14. We believe that the entertainment industry is more a catalyst than a reflection of societal change.
15. We believe that the results of talent contests should be decided by specially selected judges, not by the audience or the public.
16. We condemn the influence of the music industry on today's youth.
17. We would ban child performers in circuses.
18. We would ban the fashion industry from using Size Zero models.
19. We would ban the use of animals for entertainment.

20. We would punish sports teams whose fans misbehave.
21. We would scrap the Public Entertainment Licence in Singapore.

AFTERWORD

THIS BOOK HAS BEEN a labour of love for me, in many ways. I have accumulated a lot of knowledge about debate from my years in this field, and I have tried my best to distil it into the 11 chapters of this book. The book has hopefully taught you how to debate and argue effectively. The key lessons are useful outside of debate as well and can be applied in any conversation or written work. I urge you to experiment and apply the fundamentals in your life as well. Constant practise is the only way to improve.

Debating has been an amazing and life-changing journey for me. I hope it is the same for you, too.

GAURAV KEERTHI
gaurav@debates.org.sg

ACKNOWLEDGMENTS

THIS BOOK WOULD NOT have been possible without the support, encouragement, advice, and contributions of the following people. I owe them all a debt of gratitude.

To my family: My dad, for being an eager sparring partner over dinner every week; my mum, for putting up with all my quirks and loving me unfailingly; and my brother, for being one of my best friends as much as he is my brother.

To my closest friends and debate comrades who helped me develop many of the ideas in this book: Chan Yong Wei, Vishal Harnal, Jon Pflug, Vikram Nair, Aaron Maniam, Nabil Mustafiz, Ashraf Safdar, Ben Teo, Kelvin Tan, Tan Wu Meng, and many, many others. I wish I could fill the pages with the names of all the debaters who have touched my life in one way or other, but that would make for a very long book.

To the past and present executive committee members of Debate Association (Singapore): Thank you all for putting in the time, energy, and passion. The hard work of volunteers sometimes goes without explicit gratitude from the beneficiaries, but I'm happy all of you still know how worthwhile your efforts are.

To the WSDC 07 Singapore Team (Scott, Jon, Sam, Dana, and April) who made it to the Grand Finals against all odds: I am proud to have been part of your lives and your debate training. My memories of our collective exhilaration will never fade.

To the many young Singaporean debaters I have taught, coached (especially my DEP kids) and judged over the past decade: I have learnt more from you than you may have learnt from me.

To Mrs Lim Lai Cheng (principal of Raffles Institution), Rosie Smith, and my fellow Raffles Debate Academy Fellows: Thank you for believing in the importance of debate, and for sharing my vision of making every student a debater.

To all the local and international debaters, coaches, and judges I have interacted with, who have unknowingly helped shape my thoughts on debating.

To Melvin and Justin from Marshall Cavendish, who infused this book with their skills, time, and enthusiasm.

And finally, to you, the reader: Thank you for discovering debate. I wish you the best of luck.

"'We are all debaters,' says Gaurav. How true. In school or at the work-place, in business or in government, we are continually engaged in debate. I recommend this lucidly written book to all those who need to analyse complex issues, make robust arguments, or persuade others to their point of view."

RAVI MENON
Permanent Secretary, Ministry of Trade and Industry

"A comprehensive guide to the art of debating, sprinkled with analogies and anecdotes that show how debating skills are used in many areas of life. The book is a very useful guide for competitive debaters, and also a worthwhile read for anyone with an interest in public speaking, persuasive communication, and developing and structuring logical arguments."

MARK GABRIEL
Chief Adjudicator World Schools Debating Championships 2007

"Debating, at its most well-known, is about interrogating life's big ideas and pushing them to their logical limits, in as engaging and persuasive a manner as possible. These ideas can be intimidating for the new debater. Gaurav's book fills this need – providing bite-sized tips before fledgling speakers move on to ideas that, one hopes, will grow ever-larger as their debating journeys unfurl."

AARON MANIAM
Chief Adjudicator, World Schools Debating Championships 2008

"Gaurav provides a practical introduction to a skill that has broad applicability beyond just debate competitions. Pick up this book, and then grow into debating with your school, your friends and family."

JONATHAN PFLUG
Best Speaker, World Schools Debating Championships 2001

"This books reads like a good debate: well-structured, eloquent and entertaining! I highly recommend it to debaters and to all who wish to use debate in their life for greater success."

PEGGY PAO
Former President, Oxford Union Debate Selection Committee

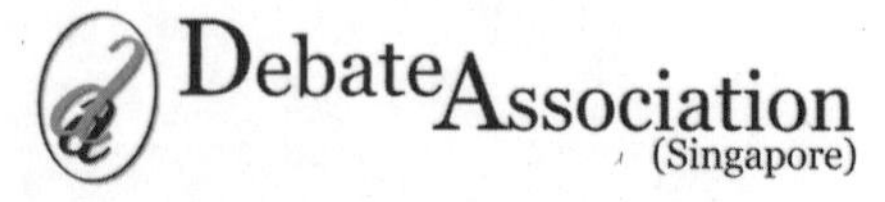

Visit the website at www.debates.org.sg